BAKE
DELICIOUSLY!™
GLUTEN & DAIRY FREE COOKBOOK

Jean Duane
Alternative Cook, LLC™

Praise for

BAKE DELICIOUSLY!™

GLUTEN AND DAIRY FREE COOKBOOK

———◆———

"When I met Jean five years ago, I was really impressed with her creative solutions to baking without dairy. Now that she has turned her talents to gluten-free baking, I am completely in awe. Not only have all of the recipes been meticulously planned and tested, but they come from a positive and generous spirit. There is no deprivation in Jean Duane's world; there is just great-tasting food."

Cindy Gawel, Pastry Chef/Owner, Bête Noire Chocolates

"Bake Deliciously! Gluten and Dairy Free will make you reevaluate what you thought you knew about GFCF diets! Jean Duane's innovative ideas, paired with taste-bud tingling images, will inspire you to set off on a culinary journey that your whole family can take part in. From cheesecake to cheese crackers, apple pie to pizza, this cookbook transforms dietary limits into options. With Jean's guidance, the GFCF lifestyle can be one that provides infinite food choices as well as a more healthful way of life for all involved."

Kelly Gilpin, Editorial Director, Future Horizons

"Bake Deliciously! Gluten and Dairy Free is a great source of recipes using healthier ingredients and methods to make them nutritious — lower in cholesterol and encourages the use of healthier GF grains. I love that all the recipes are easily made using very few steps. This is a great book for anyone new to gluten-free, dairy-free baking."

Cynthia Kupper, RD, Executive Director, Gluten Intolerance Group of North America

"Bake Deliciously! Gluten and Dairy Free provides a wealth of information about many different ingredients. It is a good reference book that answers many questions. It meets many markets for special needs including vegan. I really like the photos of the products using different ingredients to give the user an idea what happens when you alter a product's ingredients. The book offers a wide variety of baked goods, breads and breakfast items which will leave the consumer satisfied with many delicious choices that are comparable to traditional recipes. The photos of the products look appetizing and enticing to prepare."

Renee Zonka, CEC, RD, CHE, MBA, Associate Dean of Culinary/Kendall College

"Once again, Jean Duane makes cooking for our kids and adults on the Autism spectrum simple, easy and tasty too! With step-by-step instructions, baking gluten-free and dairy-free has never been this fun. If you're looking for a passionate and delicious way to connect with those you love, this is a MUST READ!"

Karen Simmons, Founder & CEO, Autism Today; Co-Author, Chicken Soup for the Soul, Children with Special Needs

"For many, baking without gluten and dairy feels like an adventure in baking blindfolded. We try, we fail, we give up and go without…without all those baked goodies that once ignited our taste buds and sent delicious shivers through our senses. Well crave no more! Illuminating the way through this world of unusual ingredients and even more unusual combinations comes Jean Duane, the Alternative Cook, with a tantalizing array of delicious GFCF baked goods. From chocolate cookies to light, delicate cakes, scrumptious breakfast treats to yummy everyday breads, these easy and fool-proof recipes will restore your faith (and confidence) in baking again. True to her name, Jean teaches us that indeed, 'there is always an alternative!'"

Veronica Zysk, Managing Editor, Autism Asperger's Digest magazine

BAKE
DELICIOUSLY!™
GLUTEN & DAIRY FREE COOKBOOK

Breads, muffins, pizza, focaccia, pies, cakes, cookies, custards, crackers, soufflés, chocolate and much more!

EMPHASIZING WHOLE, UNPROCESSED FOODS

Most recipes do not contain soy, yeast, cholesterol, refined sugar, egg yolks, dyes, artificial ingredients, artificial flavors or artificial sweeteners. Most recipes show substitutions for common allergens, and many show illustrations of the different outcomes with substitutions.

Recipes made in a few easy steps.

Jean Duane
Alternative Cook, LLC™

Bake Deliciously! Gluten and Dairy Free Cookbook

© Alternative Cook, LLC

Library of Congress Control Number: Available upon request.
Library of Congress Cataloging-in-Publication Data
Alternative Cook, LLC

ISBN: 978-0-9787109-0-3
Printed in the United States of America
First Edition, 2010

Instruction, methods, meals and foods presented in media by the Alternative Cook, LLC is not specific to any one individual's medical condition or circumstance and should not be construed as a medical diagnosis or treatment for a particular ailment or condition. Nor should such content be deemed a substitute for professional medical advice. Although the author and publisher have exhaustively researched many sources to ensure the accuracy and completeness of the information in this book, we assume no responsibility for errors, inaccuracies, omissions, or any inconsistency herein. Recipes are designed to be followed exactly as written. Substitutions may or may not yield desired results. The content and instruction provided through Alternative Cook, LLC are intended for informational purposes only and should not deter or delay your seeking medical advice and attention from a qualified medical practitioner. You are strongly urged to seek medical advice before beginning any new dietetic regimen. You are urged to seek an "approved" food list from your nutritionist and doctor for your individual condition and to follow it diligently. Ingredients on processed foods can change without warning. It is very important to read all ingredient lists each time, before consumption, to ascertain whether a product fits within your recommended dietary guidelines and is on your "approved food list". Cross-contamination is also a concern. Ensure that a manufacturer takes precautions against cross-contamination before using their product.

SUMMARY

1. Wheat-free, gluten-free, dairy-free, casein and lactose free, GFCF, Autism, Celiac cookbook
2. Baking.

For information and ordering, contact Alternative Cook, LLC, www.alternativecook.com.

Publisher: Alternative Cook, LLC™
               8200 S. Quebec Street, Suite A3-220
               Centennial, CO 80112

Dedication

Everyday when I enter into my "test kitchen" to write recipes, I say a little prayer:

"Dear Lord, please guide me today to develop delicious recipes
to help people on special diets.
Thank you for the skills you have given me."

"A forlorn and shipwrecked brother, seeing, shall take heart again."
Longfellow

This book is dedicated to you.

Contents

 ## Cakes and Cupcakes

Truffles, Brownies and Bars

Desserts

 # Cookies

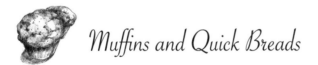 # Muffins and Quick Breads

 *Breads, Buns, Pizza, Focaccia*

 Snacks

 Breakfast Treats

Tarts, Pies and Crisps

 *Elementary Essentials*

Acknowledgements

No project like this is ever accomplished without the support and help from others. I would like to thank Mark, my beloved husband and champion in life.

My Circle of Love – Jana, Cathy, Shellie, Leslie, Kelley, Teri, Cynthia C., Cynthia H., Tammy, Tracy and Judi – gathered around me to help make Alternative Cook a success. My deepest appreciation flows from my heart to yours. Your vision and leadership are inspirational. Your undying belief in me keeps me true to my course; your support keeps me motivated.

Thanks to my mom for taking the challenge long ago to cook a heart-healthy diet for my dad. Your courage to cook with alternative ingredients set me on this lifelong path.

Thank you, Veronica Zysk, for editing this cookbook proving once again that two heads are better than one. I sincerely appreciate your insight and ideas.

Thank you, Jill Hadley, for designing and laying out this book. You've added a lot, and I sincerely appreciate your creativity and ideas. And thank you, Jack Hadley, for the beautiful line drawings and chapter icons.

A special thanks to Carol for being my mentor and friend.

And thank you, Scott. Alternative Cook would not exist without you.

The recipes in this cookbook were tested by a number of people to ensure their perfection. Thanks go out to Becky and Abby Rees, Shellie Rosser, Sue Durfee, Barbara Rodgers, Leslie Ellis, Betty Duane, Cindy Gawel, Anna Sobaski and Teri Scott for your feedback and suggestions.

I would also like to thank the numerous people I have met over the past couple of years at conferences and presentations around the country, and those who have attended my cooking demonstrations at Whole Foods and Vitamin Cottage Natural Grocers, or have contacted me through the Internet. Your wonderful ideas and requests have been incorporated into this cookbook.

It is my sincere hope that this cookbook and other media created by Alternative Cook feed not just the body but the soul of people embarking on a gluten-free, dairy-free, allergy-free lifestyle. Celebrate the abundance of great food awaiting your discovery!

ALTERNATIVE COOK, LLC™

ABOUT

Jean Duane

ALTERNATIVE COOK

Jean Duane knows first-hand what it is like to live with food intolerances. Early in life, she discovered she was dairy intolerant. In mid-life, she learned she was gluten intolerant and embarked on a journey that required her to totally change the way she cooked, ate, and lived. She maintains a gluten-free, dairy-free, low cholesterol diet, and has been developing alternative recipes for 20 years.

Jean is passionate about cooking and baking! Her mission in life is to teach others that "living without" doesn't mean having to give up eating delicious foods. Yes, you *can* have it all and still be GFCF! She focuses on using healthy, whole unprocessed foods including beans, grains, vegetables, fruits, nuts and of course, chocolate. Jean shares how to prepare fun and easy meals and baked goods with alternative ingredients the whole family can enjoy – foods that rival those made with traditional ingredients.

In addition to an MBA from the University of Colorado, Jean has been formally trained in cooking and baking, having received certification from the School of Natural Cookery. She is a member of the International Association of Culinary Professionals, and is a featured speaker and cooking demonstrator at venues around the country.

Jean Duane is a national award-winning entrepreneur, guest TV cook, author, and food evangelist. Her epicurean adventures extend to the creation of fun-packed, informative, instructional cooking DVDs and online media, including video streams. Her cooking demonstrations are available for view on Comcast's Video on Demand and PBS's *Life Wise* series.

A prolific writer, Jean has contributed articles on living and cooking GFCF to print and online publications across the country: *Scott-Free Newsletter, Autism Asperger's Digest, Gluten-Free Living, Living Without, Celiac Disease Foundation Newsletter, Gluten Intolerant Group Newsletter,* and *Denver Business Journal,* among others. She maintains an active and extensive website, **www.alternativecook.com,** offering education and inspiration to people living a GFCF lifestyle.

"Remember, there is always an alternative." ™

Foreword

"Bake deliciously and remember there is always an alternative." That's how Jean introduces her cookbook and every page lives up to her promise. Driven by her personal experiences and her professional training in cooking with natural foods, Jean offers more than 150 recipes covering a wide variety of delicious baked goods. Not only are they free of the common allergens of gluten and dairy, Jean suggests substitutions for other allergens, such as eggs and soy. And, her recipes feature whole, unprocessed ingredients as well.

Got a sweet tooth? You'll find cakes, cookies, pies and much more here. Her recipes are perfect for every occasion, whether it's for your family or special dinner guests. The Orange Cream Pie is absolutely fabulous and delivers creaminess, crunchy texture, and fresh, citrus flavors–an unbeatable combination.

Need your daily bread? Jean offers quick breads like muffins and popovers and yeast breads like French bread, focaccia, and pizza. Many of the recipes feature a wide variety of wholesome grains – sorghum, quinoa, amaranth, teff and others – that supply important nutrients for our gluten-free diet.

Jean supplements this wonderful array of recipes with vital, helpful information: how to stock a gluten-free pantry, what different ingredients do in baking, and definitions of the techniques she uses in this book. This information is especially important if you're new to the gluten-free diet or don't have much prior experience in baking.

If you're looking for delicious GFCF baked goods that will "fool" even the most discriminating palate, this book is for you. Go get a copy and start baking. You will soon become a true believer in Jean's promise: *there is always an alternative."*

Carol Fenster, author of 1,000 Gluten-Free Recipes and Gluten-Free Quick & Easy

—◆—

LIVING A GLUTEN-FREE AND CASEIN-FREE LIFESTYLE

I spent years "bellyaching" – literally. Every night I had a stomachache. Time and time again, I sought help from doctors who told me a variety of things, including that my pain was "in my head" and that I had an "interesting intestinal configuration." For years I bought that as the reason for my digestive maladies, took a host of digestive aids and suffered through intrusive tests.

From an early age I was dairy intolerant, but despite my careful avoidance of dairy products, I still never felt well. It wasn't until I developed an awful, itchy rash in 2003 that doctors started taking me seriously. The rash landed me in the emergency room the first time. Doctors proclaimed it was a "systemic chemical reaction" and a "histamine reaction." But, even after more tests nobody knew what was causing it. *Two years* later, a new-to-me doctor suggested wheat. Further tests were done and a protein called gluten seemed to be the culprit. Gluten? Wasn't that bread – the staff of life? It seemed sacrilegious to me and very difficult to accept that the food revered in the Bible, the very manna of God, was poison to my body. And all those years feeling ill – what took so many doctors so long to suspect gluten?

Since that fateful day, I've become much more informed about gluten with a much more positive outlook toward my health and my relationship with food. I know now I had gluten intolerance years before I reached my "threshold", when the rash appeared, and that other signs were there all along. I just didn't know what to look for, and apparently, neither did most of the medical professionals I sought out. Thankfully I did find someone knowledgeable, and as a result, was diagnosed with "symptoms congruous with dermatitis herpetiformis", a form of Celiac Disease that manifests on the skin. (Pretty impressive name, wouldn't you agree?)

At first I was afraid to eat anything. It seemed like virtually every morsel of food I was used to eating contained gluten. The more I read the more I discovered contradictory information about what did and did not contain gluten. I became wary about everything I put into my mouth. Fortunately, I was attending cooking school at the time of diagnosis, and that educational environment helped me learn quickly. I was also incredibly motivated! After years of suffering, I was ready, willing and able to finally fight the invisible enemy that had dogged me for so long.

My non-baking husband didn't fare as well through this transition. I was no longer baking the favorite recipes he used to enjoy, and he felt deprived. Who wouldn't? I felt deprived too. As a measure of compromise, I wrote a list of the things I used to bake for him; posted it on the refrigerator, and once a week I baked a gluten-containing favorite of his choice. We continued this way for the first six months post-diagnosis. You can imagine my surprise when I returned to my doctor and found out my blood tests didn't improve. It turned out that simply breathing gluten while baking, just a speck of it, was enough to cause problems.

Being the rebel I am, I refused to accept that living without gluten meant my husband and I would forever be relegated to "living without" – without all the delicious foods and baked goods we enjoyed so much. With my culinary background and a dedicated resolve, I started experimenting in the kitchen, developing gluten-free, dairy-free recipes. My husband is no longer deprived of his favorite foods, and neither am I. We eat scrumptious cakes and pies, cookies, snacks, and breakfast treats – all rivaling (and sometimes tasting better than) the gluten-filled varieties.

The good news is you don't ever have to feel deprived again either. *Bake Deliciously!* is the culmination of years of tests and trials, flops and feasts, and contains foolproof recipes that will restore your love of baking! Here you'll find delicious, nutritious and easy-to-make baked goods that satisfy your cravings for "homemade." Recipes are triple-tested so you can bake to your heart's content, assured of success every time. And, all of the recipes support guidelines for several different special diets: the GFCF Diet, the Celiac Diet, the Gluten Intolerant Diet, the Lactose Intolerant Diet, and the Heart Healthy Diet.

Yes, at first this will be an adventure into the unknown. It was that way for me and it is that way for anyone embarking on learning to cook, bake and live without gluten and/or dairy. You'll need to become familiar with alternative foods – foods you may never have heard of before: sorghum flour, xanthan gum, agar, guar gum, nutritional yeast and teff, to name a few. But, hey, gluten was an unfamiliar word when we first heard it too! After you use these new ingredients a few times they'll seem normal in your pantry. With a little time and attention, these "unusual" combinations won't seem so weird anymore. For example, you might see recipes for sweet baked goods with vinegar added! *Vinegar?* You'll learn that vinegar balances the pH in some recipes and activates leavening. The basic "chemistry" of baking GFCF will become second nature. And even if it doesn't, no worries! You'll have this arsenal of surefire recipes at your fingertips whenever the urge to bake hits you!

Even better, you just might notice that some of these new foods are actually *more* compatible to your body system. Nutritionists are always advising us to eat a variety of foods and there is quite a variety to choose from when baking GFCF! Rich creamy custards and milks can be made from nuts or seeds. The typical bleached, refined white wheat flour will be replaced with nutritious flours made from whole grains, beans, nuts, seeds, and even vegetables. The most amazing thing of all is that most people will not be able to tell the difference between foods made with traditional ingredients and those made with alternative ingredients! My husband, friends and family can't tell – in fact, they request many of my baked goods now! Baking "without" doesn't sound so bad after all, does it?

Bake Deliciously! will help you through this transition to a new, healthier way of eating and baking. Once you get the hang of baking without certain foods, you'll become an empowered cook. Using the information and tools in this cookbook, you'll learn how to convert your favorite recipes and create new ones. You'll feel confident in bringing "look-alikes" to celebrations and gatherings with friends and family, knowing you can eat without worry. After a while of cooking "free," you'll feel so much better that nobody could pay you enough money to go back to eating those foods again.

It is my hope and prayer that you enjoy the recipes in this cookbook. It is chock-full of sweet and savory treats for special occasions as well as more common baked goods that will make every day a mini-celebration of its own. I've included some of my very favorite personal recipes that my family has feasted on for years, along with some brand new recipes for baked goods that will please even the most discriminating palate. Be brave and venture into this different way of baking, with this cookbook as your guide. With just a little time and practice, you'll be creating GFCF favorites of your own that will become treasured family traditions and feed you and yours for years to come.

Jean Duane

ALTERNATIVE COOK, LLC™

GFCF BASICS

The standard American diet, centered as it is on wheat, milk, and animal products, has not served some of us very well. Millions of people are sensitive to gluten and dairy.

* One in every 100 people in America has Celiac Disease. *(Peter H. Green, MD, 2008)*

* 90 million have some form of gluten sensitivity. *(Braly and Hoggan, 2002)*

* According to the 2008 U.S. Census, one in every 4 people cannot digest dairy.

* Some 11 million Americans suffer from food allergies *(National Institutes of Health)* and the Centers for Disease Control and Prevention asserts another 30 million have food intolerances.

* One in every 150 children born today will be diagnosed on the Autism spectrum. A gluten-free, dairy-free diet improves functioning in many of these children and adults. *(www.talkaboutcuringautism.org)*

* 102 million Americans are urged to follow a low-cholesterol diet. *(http://nutrition.ucdavis.edu/InfoSheets/ANR/CholesterolFact.pdf)*

* "Clean Eating" athletes find their performance improves on a gluten-free, dairy-free diet. *(Sports and Fitness Magazine, October, 2007)*

* Nursing mothers can avert colic in their baby by eating a gluten-free, dairy-free diet. *(www.drgreene.com/21_2038.html)*

* People with Irritable Bowel Syndrome and Crohn's disease improve when following a gluten-free, dairy-free diet. *(www.celiac.com; www.irritable-bowel-syndrome.ws/gluten-free-diet.htm)*

As the number of health-challenged individuals continues to rise, it is time we all keep an open mind to the body-brain connection and realize that what we eat affects how we function. More and more people are turning to special diets as an alternative way to restore health, wellness and a sense of well-being on a physical level. Some do this by choice; others are diagnosed with conditions that mandate this change in lifestyle. Still others are doing it for their children, their health and their future.

When you think about it, eating is the second most intimate thing adults do. What you put into your mouth manifests either as good health, vigor, energy, beautiful skin, a positive outlook and a body the right size for your frame; or a feeling of malaise, puffiness, a lack of strength and vitality, chronic illness, intense cravings, pasty skin and a body too large or too small for your frame. Food may be the root cause for many chronic health problems. The right diet can lead to a thriving body and mind.

Gluten is associated with seemingly unrelated illnesses such as migraines, arthritis, sinus problems, joint pain, itchy rashes, infertility, depression, discolored teeth and a host of digestive maladies. Casein (the protein), and lactose (the sugar) found in dairy products are correlated with asthma, itchy skin, runny nose, difficulty breathing as well digestive complaints. For a subset of the youth and adult population, the proteins in nuts, soy and egg yolks are allergens. Others find sugar wreaks havoc on their bodies. It's no longer a full-fledged food allergy that brings about health complications. Today, many individuals have food intolerances that cause serious health problems.

I have been fortunate to speak at and attend conferences across the country addressing Autism, Celiac Disease and gluten intolerance. Over and over, people share stories of how a gluten-free, casein-free (GFCF) diet has helped them regain health. Parents of Autistic children and adults on the spectrum overwhelmingly report the positive benefits of eliminating gluten and casein from their diet. Spaced-out children living in a daily fog have become alert and attentive within days of removing gluten. Digestive irregularities clear up for the first time in a child's life. Language emerges where no language existed before. Stimming (repetitive body movement) subsides. The results are often remarkable and sustainable.

Food holds a deeply intimate place in our culture. It's not just about eating and nourishment. Preparing and eating food is a social experience for many of us, and restrictions affect not just our physical health, but our sense of belonging, of friendship, culture and family. *Baking* without gluten and casein can be the most challenging part of this lifestyle. The success of baked goods is largely dependent upon certain types of ingredients combined in specific proportions. Leave something out, or make a wrong substitute and the entire recipe collapses.

However challenging it may be, in the end I believe health is worth the effort. With a little time and ingenuity, we can keep our social lifestyles and be gluten and casein free in our diets. So, please don't give up too soon if this lifestyle is proving to be a challenge for you. Seek out help (and this cookbook!) before throwing in the kitchen towel. It may take several months to experience physical improvements, but in the long run, it is certainly worth it to thrive!

ABOUT GLUTEN

Unfortunately, the Food and Drug Administration (FDA) only requires food manufacturers to state the top eight allergens on label ingredients lists. So, while "wheat" will probably be listed, often "gluten" is not. And this can be disastrous for those who are so sensitive to gluten that even a tiny bit can hurt.

Other than the general rule to avoid anything with wheat in its name, you'll need to learn a few others names for gluten. Gluten is naturally present in a plethora of items eaten regularly in the typical American diet. Some things with gluten in them are easy to spot, like whole wheat bread. Others are a surprise, like bouillon cubes or mustard powder. The following list is an introduction to learning the other names for gluten, and items that contain gluten. It's a starting point, not an exhaustive list. Please investigate any ingredient you suspect contains foods you are avoiding.

OTHER NAMES FOR GLUTEN

Abyssinian hard

Avena (oats)

Barley; barley hordeum vulgare; barley malt

Bran

Bulgur

Couscous

Durum

Edible starch (unless source is disclosed)

Einkorn wheat

Farina

Fu (dried wheat gluten/Japanese)

Germ; wheat germ

Glutamate; glutamic acid

Hordeum

Hydrolyzed oat starch (unless specifically from gluten-free oats)

Hydrolyzed plant protein

Hydrolyzed vegetable protein/HVP

Job's tears (ancient form of barley)

Kamut

Malt of any kind (vinegar, liquor/from barley)

Modified food starch (unless source is disclosed)

Monosodium glutamate/MSG (unless made in the U.S.)

Oats and oatmeal (unless specifically labeled gluten-free)

Rye

Seitan (pure gluten protein)

Semolina

Semolina triticum

Spelt

Spelt triticum spelta

Starch (unless source is disclosed)

Tritical

Tritical X Tritic

Osecale

Triticum

Vital gluten

Wheat durum triticum

Wheat triticum aestivum

Wheat triticum mononoccum

ALTERNATIVE COOK, LLC™

"HIDDEN" SOURCES OF GLUTEN

Gluten can be hiding in many common items you'd never think contain the culprit! Always check ingredients, even on things you wouldn't normally associate with gluten. My doctor tells me the skin absorbs around 30% of what is put on it, so soaps, lotions and makeup are off limits if they contain gluten. Hairspray containing "wheat protein" can find its way into the body through the lungs and possibly through the scalp.

Baking powder

Baking soda

Beer (gluten-free beer is available)

Bouillon cubes/powders

Communion wafers

Craft paste

Detergents

Glue on postage stamps, envelopes and kids' stickers

Ground spices

Hairspray

Make-up, lipstick/lip balms

Miso (may be made with barley or other gluten-containing grains)

Mustard powder

Play-dough

Prescription and over-the-counter medications

Shampoo

Sunscreen (little kids often put their hands in their mouths)

Tempeh (usually made only from soy, but may be made with multiple grains)

Tofu (usually made only from soy, but may be made with multiple grains)

Toothpaste and mouthwashes

Vegetable broth

Vitamins and other supplements

ABOUT DAIRY

When milk is separated, the result is curds and whey (remember the poem about Little Miss Muffet?) Curds are the solid protein, called casein. Whey is the liquid part of milk, which contains the milk sugar, lactose. Whey is used to make cheese, and as a supplement for body builders. Lactose is broken down with the enzyme lactase, which is available over the counter in tablet form. Some people who are lactose intolerant can eat dairy products if they eat a lactase tablet with it. Others with a dairy allergy/intolerance may be reacting to the protein, casein. People avoiding dairy need to be aware of all three of these components as well as a host of other names that indicate a food is derived from milk. Be on the lookout for foods that contain any of the following ingredients.

OTHER NAMES FOR DAIRY

Acidophilus milk

Butter

Butter oil

Buttermilk

Calcium caseinate

Calcium stearoyl lactylate

Cheese

Curds

Galactose

Ghee

Hydrolysates

Lactalbumin

Lactalbumin phosphate

Lactic acid (may be derived from sour milk or whey)

Lacto globulin

Lactose

Magnesium caseinate

Potassium caseinate

Rennet casein

Sodium lactylate

Whey, in any form including delactosed, isolate, protein concentrate

ALTERNATIVE COOK, LLC™

"HIDDEN" SOURCES OF DAIRY

Artificial coffee whiteners/creamers

Artificial sweeteners (some)

Breath mints/chewing gum

Butter flavoring

Canned tuna (some varieties use hydrolyzed caseinate)

Caramel coloring

Certain flavors of candy, jellybeans and gumdrops (caramel, pina colada, etc.)

Chicken broth

Fat replacers

Imitation syrups/flavorings

Luncheon meats

Natural chocolate flavoring

Prescription medications (often use casein and/or lactose as a binder)

Sherbet (most sorbets are dairy-free, but many sherbets have a dairy component)

Slicers used at deli counters (often the same slicer is used for meat and cheese)

Soy "meat" products

Spice mixes

Turkey

INGREDIENTS CHANGE: LABEL READING

Anyone who has embarked on the journey to remove gluten and/or casein from their diets knows it is a constant endeavor. Label reading becomes second nature; calling manufacturers to check current recipes and ingredients a common occurrence. Most manufacturers list an 800 number and *usually* the person on the other end of the phone knows what gluten or casein is. Or, contact the manufacturer through their website and ask your question via email. I've had some interesting experiences – people who interchanged the words glucose and gluten during the conversation, which diminishes their credibility, to say the least. Whether you call or email, it's wise to screen the person on the other end before blindly accepting what he or she tells you. Try asking a couple of questions to which you already know the answer. It will tell you much about trusting their answers.

A few name-brand ingredients are recommended in this cookbook. Alternative Cook is not sponsored by anyone; these are just foods I like and that work in the recipes. At the time the cookbook was written, these ingredients were gluten and dairy-free. Sadly, we can't rest assured that a gluten-free product one month is still gluten-free the next. Food manufacturing companies are notorious for modifying their formulas at any given time, or changing ingredients based on what is inexpensive and available. Check and re-check. Read ingredients each time you purchase a product.

STOCKING YOUR PANTRY WITH GLUTEN-FREE / CASEIN-FREE ALTERNATIVES

There's no shortage of options when cooking or baking free of gluten and/or casein. Most ingredients can be found (or ordered) through a local natural food store, or food store chains. If those options are not available in your area, never fear! There are numerous online sources for common and more obscure GFCF food items.

One of my favorite activities is going to the natural food store. It is such a positive sensory experience. I love the smell of the store when I walk in and see the beautiful array of fruits and vegetables on display. The ingredients on the shelf pique my curiosity and imagination, and I usually leave with something unfamiliar in my bag. It's fun to figure out its properties and how to incorporate it into different recipes. Developing this cookbook led me to experiment with several proteins, such as soy protein isolate, hemp seed protein and rice protein. In the process, I found what worked and what didn't in recipes.

My idea of a good time is to find an ingredient and turn it into something new – to go where no cook has gone before. In this book, you'll find a recipe for **Whipped Cream** (Page 89) made from soy protein isolate and a new way of making **"Margarine"** (Page 213) – inventions from these exploratory trials.

There is an abundance of foods available to us, even on a restrictive diet. I particularly like going to natural food stores because they go to great lengths to ensure the ingredients carried meet their definition of healthy. For me, that's a green light to try it, or experiment with it. If it is available in the health food store, (and it is gluten and dairy free) I generally consider it to be a food I would incorporate into my diet.

Anyone serious about baking without gluten and casein needs a pantry stocked with the more frequently used ingredients. It saves time and frustration. There's nothing more disappointing than getting ready to try a new recipe, or finding a free hour to bake a batch of bread only to discover that one essential item is missing from your pantry. The ingredients that follow with an asterisk are the "workhorses" of the Alternative Cook's kitchen.

Gluten-Free Grain Flours

Amaranth flour

Brown rice flour*

Buckwheat flour*

Cornmeal*

Millet flour

Popcorn flour

Quinoa flour

Sorghum flour*

Teff flour*

Gluten-Free Protein Flours

Acorn flour

Almond meal*

Fava bean flour

Gafava bean flour*

Garbanzo bean flour*

Hazelnut meal

Navy bean flour

Pea flour

Pecan meal

Pinto bean flour

Potato flour

Sesame seed flour

Soy flour*

Sunflower seed flour

Walnut meal

White bean flour*

Vegetable Flours

Artichoke flour

Ground (freeze-dried) vegetables*

Sweet potato flour

Water chestnut flour

Alternative Starches

Arrowroot*

Cornstarch*

Kudzu*

Potato starch*

Tapioca starch (a.k.a. Tapioca flour)*

Taro flour (starch)

Expandex™

Sweeteners

Agave nectar*

Blackstrap molasses*

Date sugar*

Florida Crystals®

Honey

Maple sugar*

Organic cane sugar*

Stevia*

Sucanat®*

Fats

Almond butter*

Olive oil*

Peanut butter*

Raw tahini butter*

Spray-on oil (GF)*

Sunflower oil*

Walnut oil*

Stabilizers/Binders

Agar powder* or flakes

Guar gum*

Flax seeds*

Just Whites® (dried egg whites)*

Kudzu*

Xanthan gum*

Milks

Raw nuts* (almonds, pecans, walnuts) or seeds (hemp or sunflower) to make your own "milk" for a recipe

Rice milk, plain and vanilla varieties*

Other

Active dry yeast*

Apple cider vinegar*

Baking powder*

Baking soda*

Chocolate chips (Tropical Source are gluten and dairy-free)

Chocolate bars (Scharffen Berger 70% or Tropical Source)

Cream of tartar*

GF rice, corn or millet cereals*

Gluten-free oats*

Liquid lecithin*

Nutritional yeast*

Salt*

Soy protein isolate*

Sparkling water*

EQUIPMENT

Having the right tools for the job can make GFCF baking easier and more fun! While some of these items are not required to complete the recipes, in most cases having this equipment will save you time and make baking a breeze. I've listed the size pan that I use for a recipe, but there is no need to run out and buy a baking pan that matches the size exactly. Using "medium" sized baking pans work for most recipes.

Assorted mixing bowls, measuring cups and spoons

Blender

Cookie press

Docker (for making crackers)

Food processor

Hand mixer

Parchment paper

Pastry bag and tips

Silpat (a silicone non-stick baking mat)

Stand mixer with a paddle and a whisk attachment

COMMONLY USED GLUTEN-FREE INGREDIENTS

Arrowroot is a powdered starch made from the arrowroot plant. It is tasteless and is typically used as a thickening agent for sauces, puddings, glazes and fruit pie fillings. It is considered a whole food and is said to balance the pH in the body.

Agar powder / flakes. Agar (or agar agar) is a white, semi-translucent vegetarian gelatin derived from seaweed. It is also known as kanten (in Japan) and as China Grass (in India). It is used as a thickening agent in soups, jellies and desserts. It comes in various forms: sticks, which must be melted in water before using; as flakes, or in powdered form (which is preferred). It can be purchased in Asian markets.

Amaranth is an ancient grain that is highly nutritious, containing large amounts of protein and amino acids. It is a good source of dietary fiber and minerals. For fun sometime, try popping it like popcorn.

Baking Powder. Baking powder is made of three components: an acid which is usually cream of tartar, a base which is baking soda, and filler which is usually cornstarch. You can easily make your own baking powder by mixing 2 TBS Cream of Tartar, 1 TBS baking soda and 1 TBS cornstarch. If you purchase baking powder, just be sure the filler is gluten-free.

Baking Soda. Baking soda is often used instead of baking powder when the recipe already contains an acid such as lemon juice, vinegar, cocoa powder or tomato juice. A form of salt, baking soda is naturally gluten-free.

Bean flours are just that: flours made from various varieties of cooked beans. The benefits of using bean flours are many: they add protein, fiber and iron; have no cholesterol; and make the final product a little lighter. For best results, use up to 25% bean flours in a recipe; garbanzo, fava, soy, white bean, navy or pinto bean flour work well in baked goods. Bean flours made from processed beans make the best baked items.

Beet powder. Beet powder is made from dehydrated ripe red beets ground into a powder. It can be used in soups and sauces, as an ingredient in homemade pasta, and as a natural food dye.

Brown rice flour is a whole grain flour and is a staple in the alternative kitchen. Some manufacturers grind whole grain rice flour more finely than do others. For example, Authentic Food's brown rice flour is finely ground and therefore yields a smoother textured item than does Bob's Red Mill's whole grain brown rice flour, which is a slightly coarser grind. Both produce lovely baked items, depending on the texture and outcome you desire.

Buckwheat, in spite of its name, is not derived from wheat. It is a grass. Buckwheat flour adds a distinctive taste and light texture to baked goods.

Citric acid. Gluten-free baking requires an acid to balance the mixture's pH and activate the leavening and citric acid is sometimes used for this. Citric acid is also used as a preservative in foods. Look for it in the supplement section in the natural food store or online.

Corn flour is the finest grind of the corn kernel. Cornmeal is a coarser, medium grind, and grits are the coarsest grind of corn. Masa Harina is corn processed with lime or lye, ground finely and is commonly used for tortillas, tamales and in other Mexican dishes.

Date sugar is an unprocessed sweetener made from dehydrated and finely ground dates. It is high in fiber, but does not dissolve in liquids.

Dried fruit. Dried fruit is used in some recipes. Try to find "un-sulfured" dried fruit. (The sulfur imparts an undesirable taste in foods.) Also, be sure the dried fruit – especially raisins and date pieces – is gluten-free. Some processing plants dust their conveyor belts or the fruit with flour to prevent dried fruits from sticking together. This sometimes applies to raisins packaged in canisters, so please check!

Expandex™ is modified tapioca starch, used in place of tapioca starch or tapioca flour. It enhances the appearance, texture and flavor of baked goods, and creates a crumb texture similar to that of wheat-based items.

Flaked grains. In addition to gluten-free flaked oats, you can also purchase other flaked grains such as buckwheat, quinoa or rice flakes. Flaked grains cook more quickly than their rolled counterparts and work well in baked goods for both flavor and texture.

Florida Crystals®. This company presses juice from the sugar cane, purifies and crystallizes it so the sugar is somewhat less processed than refined sugar. Animal bones, typically used in refining ordinary white sugar, are not used in making Florida Crystals®. The recipes in this book suggesting Florida Crystals® are referring to the granulated (white) sugar. Organic cane sugar can be used instead.

Flax Seeds. Brown or golden flax seed are used as an egg replacement when ground up with water. Ground flax seeds are also used in recipes to add fiber and omega 3 fatty acids.

Gafava flour is a blend of garbanzo and fava flour. If you cannot locate the mixture, you could make your own by blending equal parts of the two flours, or just use one or the other.

Guar gum. See listing under xanthan gum.

Hemp seeds. Like flax seeds, they are full of essential amino acids and essential fatty acids. The seeds can be eaten raw, ground into a meal or made into hemp milk. They are a healthy, tasty alternative for people avoiding nuts.

Kudzu is a starch-like thickener, similar to cornstarch, arrowroot or potato starch. Dissolved in water or liquid and heated, kudzu will become clear and add stickiness or thickening to a mixture.

Lecithin. Lecithin is made from soy and is used as an emulsifier in its liquid form, and as a dough enhancer in its granular form. It is also used as an egg substitute when mixed with oil.

Lemon oil is derived from the zest of the lemon (the yellow part of the rind). It can be purchased at gourmet food and kitchen supply stores. Williams Sonoma carries McNess Pure Lemon Oil, a brand I love to use in baking. The amount of oil used depends on the level of concentration, taste, and pungency of the various brands. Start off with a few drops and adjust to taste. (Note: please be sure to buy food-grade lemon oil and not furniture polish with the same name!)

Maple sugar is the crystallized product that remains when sap is boiled down beyond maple syrup. It is considered pure. I generally substitute it one-for-one instead of sugar in recipes, but because it is sweeter than sugar, you might consider substituting two-thirds and tasting before adding more.

ALTERNATIVE COOK, LLC™

Maple syrup. Pure maple syrup is made from the sap of maple trees. It is available in the USA in grades A and B, which progress from a lighter, milder flavor in grade A (which comes in Light Amber, Medium Amber and Dark Amber) to a darker, more robust flavor in grade B.

Mayonnaise is used as a fat substitute in recipes. My favorite GFCF soy version is called Nayonaise from Nasoya®.

Montina® flour is a high-protein, high fiber grass that is ground into flour. It is available online directly from a company called Amazing Grains and can be found at some natural food stores.

Natural food coloring. If you want to naturally enhance the color of your baked goods, consider using a natural food coloring. Plant extracts are used as the basis for natural food coloring, which produce a food dye that is considered safe. Dried beet powder or black and red currents are used to make red (versus commercial red dye which is often made from beetles and called "carmine" in ingredients). Turmeric is used for yellow, parsley for green, annatto for orange, and blueberries are used for blue. Make sure whatever natural food coloring you use is gluten-free.

Nut meal adds texture and protein to baked goods. Nuts can be ground coarsely or finely depending on your taste. Some easy-to-find nut meals include almond meal, hazelnut meal and chestnut flour. For a simple recipe for nut or seed meal, please turn to Page 214.

Nutritional yeast. Nutritional yeast is a fungus grown on molasses and then pasteurized to kill the yeast cells. It is highly nutritious, with 18 amino acids, 15 minerals, and is rich in B-complex vitamins – including B12. It gives a "cheese" taste to dishes. Because it has been deactivated through pasteurization, nutritional yeast does not promote Candida growth.

Oats. Oats are naturally gluten-free, however, the way oats are grown and processed in this country results in oats being cross-contaminated by other gluten containing grains. Gluten-free oats and oatmeal are available from several manufacturers. Look for packages that specifically say the oats are gluten-free; if it doesn't, they are not. If you decide to incorporate oats into your diet (with doctor supervision) do it slowly, over time, to ensure you can tolerate them. A suggestion is to make a batch of the **Oatmeal Chocolate Raisin Cookies** (Page 102) in this cookbook. Freeze them, and eat one cookie every third day for the first two weeks. Eat two cookies every third day for two more weeks. Note how you feel each day. If you feel well, you can probably add oats to your diet. Once you are comfortable eating them, gluten-free oat manufacturers recommend limiting your intake of oats to 1½ cups per week if you follow a gluten-free or other special diet.

Orange oil is derived from the zest of an orange. The amount of oil used depends on the level of concentration, taste, and pungency of the various brands. Start off with a few drops and adjust to taste. Like its cousin lemon oil, it can be purchased at gourmet food and kitchen supply stores.

Organic cane sugar is the "first crystallized sugar" made from sugar cane juice, and as such, is less processed than refined sugar. To be certified "organic", the cane must be grown on land that is free of pesticides, herbicides and chemicals.

Potato flour, made from potatoes, is very starchy and when combined in a recipe, will add lightness to baked goods. Note: Potato starch and potato flour are not the same thing.

Potato starch. Also derived from potatoes, is a substitute thickener for flour, similar to cornstarch or kudzu. Like its counterparts, it dissolves translucently and thickens without adding a "cloudy" appearance to goods.

Powdered milk. Powdered milk is added to bread to make it tender and to add taste. GFCF powdered milk products are made from rice, soy or potatoes. The most popular brands are Better than Milk® (from soy and rice) and Vance's Darifree® (from potato).

Rice vinegar is a "soft" tasting vinegar made from fermented rice or rice wine. It is more mild and "sweet" tasting than the traditional acidic white or apple cider vinegars. There are several types of rice vinegar, with varying tastes. Recipes in this cookbook use white rice vinegar. Note: rice vinegar is not the same as "seasoned rice vinegar", which is a condiment made with sake, sugar and salt.

Seed meal. Seed meal is made from ground seeds. Easy-to-find seeds include pumpkin, flax, hemp, sunflower and sesame seeds. To grind, simply place in a food processor until it becomes a meal. Seed meal is used to boost the taste and protein content of foods. It goes rancid quickly, so it's best to grind fresh for each use.

Sorghum flour (Milo flour) is a whole-grain workhorse in the Alternative Cook's kitchen. Sorghum flour works best in combination with other gluten-free flours, but is one that can be used in a higher percentage of the total flour in baked goods. High in insoluble fibers, it is metabolized slowly, making it appealing to diabetics.

Soy flour. Soy flour is made from roasted soy beans that have been ground into a flour. Two kinds of soy flour are available – "natural" or defatted. I prefer to use the natural or full-fat flour because it is considered "whole." Soy flour can be substituted with any "bean" flour, such as navy, fava, white bean, garbanzo, or pinto bean flour.

Soy protein isolate is a purified form of soy protein, used in this cookbook as an egg replacement and a component in making a non-dairy whipped topping.

Sucanat®. A contraction of "Sugar Cane Natural," Sucanat® is pure, dried cane juice and as such, retains its natural molasses content. It is used in this cookbook in place of brown sugar because it is less refined.

Sweet rice flour is a starch derived from rice. It can be used as a thickening agent, and is often used in cakes and pies. It can be substituted with other starches.

Stevia is a natural sweetener made from the leaf of the Stevia plant, an herb native to Paraguay. It is significantly sweeter than sugar (1⁄40 of a tsp. of stevia equals the sweetness of 1 tsp. of sugar) and works well in puddings, beverages, custards and no-bake pie fillings. It is zero calories and considered zero on the glycemic index, and is often used as an alternative sweetener by diabetics and those following a Candida-reducing diet. It is available in powered or liquid form. Recipes in this cookbook call for powdered stevia with no fillers or added fiber.

Tapioca flour / Tapioca starch / Cassava starch (all the same thing) come from the yucca root (cassava plant). This finely-ground white flour/powder enhances elasticity when added to the flour mix and adds a chewy texture to baked goods.

Tahini is sesame seed butter made from either raw or roasted ground sesame seeds. Recipes in this cookbook call for raw tahini. Tahini is nutritious and is used as an alternative source of calcium.

ALTERNATIVE COOK, LLC™

Teff is among the highest protein grains and comes from Ethiopia. It is a good source of fiber, carbohydrates and calcium, and its iron content is easily absorbed by the body. It can be eaten as a grain or can be ground into flour. Considering that the world's best marathon athletes come from Ethiopia and their staple grain is teff, athletes may be well-advised to incorporate teff into their diet.

Tofu. Tofu is bean curd, usually but not always, made from soy beans. It can be purchased in different varieties: extra firm, firm, soft and extra silky. Recipes in this book specify the type to use. Tofu should not be eaten raw. When used in no-cook recipes, steam the tofu for five to ten minutes and press out the extra moisture in paper towels before using.

Ume plum vinegar. The ume plum is common in Japan. It is harvested when green and when pickled, it is called an umeboshi plum – often used as a condiment. These plums are tart and are frequently made into vinegar, jam or wine.

Vanilla. Imitation vanilla and natural vanilla flavoring are different from vanilla extract. Pure vanilla extract made from vanilla beans imparts a lovely taste in baked goods. Recipes in this cookbook call for pure vanilla extract.

Vanilla powder is a concentrated form of vanilla. It is used in recipes to boost the vanilla taste without adding more liquid to a recipe, and since it contains an emulsifier, it is particularly effective in meringues and soufflés. It is available in natural and gourmet grocery stores as well as cooking supply stores.

Vegetable broth powder. These powders add depth of flavor to many dishes. The recipes in this cookbook assume an unsalted vegetable powder is being used. If the vegetable broth powder contains salt, adjust the salt in the recipe accordingly. If you have a hard time finding a "pure" vegetable broth powder, simply purchase dehydrated vegetables (preferably without onions) and grind them in your food processor.

White bean flour is high in fiber, protein and iron. It makes baked goods lighter, and is therefore sometimes used as part of a flour combination in gluten-free cooking.

Xanthan and guar gum. These gums are used in gluten-free baking to substitute for gluten. They are available in the natural food store and online. For more information on gums, please turn to Page 18.

Xylitol is a "sugar alcohol" derived from fruits, corn, vegetables, oats or mushrooms. Usually it is made from corn (check the label for its origin). It has one-third fewer calories than sugar and is zero on the glycemic index. It is used by diabetics and those following a Candida-reducing diet. If you decide to experiment with xylitol, incorporate it slowly into the diet. Because physical systems react differently to xylitol, it should be incorporated slowly into the diet.

Yeast is a leavening agent used to convert sugar and starch into carbon dioxide bubbles and alcohol, which causes breads to rise. Yeast comes in raw cakes and dry granules in packets. The recipes in this cookbook use active dry yeast. Be sure to check expiration dates when buying yeast, and store it in the freezer to elongate its shelf life. Bring yeast to room temperature before using.

THE ART AND SCIENCE
OF BAKING GFCF

When I started baking without gluten, I analyzed hundreds of gluten-free recipes in various categories – breads, cakes, cookies, bars, etc. I developed spreadsheets to determine the breakdown and ratios of gluten-free flour combinations, and was shocked that most contained between 60-75% highly refined starch! Prior to being gluten-free, the most starch I had ever used in a recipe was 1-2 TBS, and some of these gluten-free recipes called for *cups* of various starches. Gluten-free or not, considering that highly-refined (white) foods are correlated with diabetes, heart disease, obesity and cancer, I was determined to develop baked recipes that emphasized whole foods. Interestingly, that became the impetus for this cookbook.

Gluten-free baking works best with a combination of flours – usually grain flours mixed with protein flours and starches. And, the proportions of these ingredients matter. For example, cakes and other lighter-textured baked goods require some starch, whereas beautiful muffins, cookies and quick breads can be made with little or no starch. Each recipe in this cookbook was developed with the goal of using 25% or less starch. Sometimes I attained this objective, sometimes I could not – and sometimes I developed successful recipes with all whole-grain flours.

Many gluten-free cookbooks start with a recipe for a "universal" flour mix – a combination of flours that can be made in quantities and used for most baked recipes throughout the book. You'll not find such a recipe in this cookbook, and I'll tell you why. First, I have used them before and did not like having dibs and dabs of leftover flour mixes in my freezer which were ultimately thrown away. That's just wasted time and money. Second, these "all purpose, sure-fire" flour mixes contain a surprising proportion of refined starches (tapioca flour, cornstarch, potato starch and sweet rice flour). My personal baking philosophy is to opt for maximum health and nutrition, rather than use these refined products. The flour combinations presented in each recipe in *Bake Deliciously!* represent the best combination for that specific item.

Flour mixes can also be bought pre-packaged. If you find yourself needing to save a little time, or you prefer to use a pre-packaged flour mix, simply add together the quantity of the different flours called for in the recipe's ingredients (the grain, protein and starch flours in the Dry Ingredient section of the recipe) and use that much of the off-the-shelf flour mix. For example, if a recipe in the book calls for ½ cup sorghum flour, ¼ cup gafava bean flour and ¼ cup cornstarch, substitute those with 1 cup of the all-purpose gluten-free blend and keep the rest of the recipe the same. Recipes were not tested with pre-packaged flour blends, but I would expect them to turn out satisfactorily.

Like most things, baking GFCF is a learned experience. Successful baked goods depend on certain components in certain proportions. In addition, where you live, your oven, the time of year/day you bake (high or low pressure system, cold or hot temperatures, humidity) and even the particular batch of flour will all play a role in how the baked good turns out. (Incidentally, while high-altitude does affect rising time, it doesn't seem to be a factor in gluten-free baking. I've had these recipes tested at 9,000 feet and at sea level with consistent results.) The experimental baker becomes successful through trial and error, a willingness to try the recipe numerous times, and changing only one variable to see what

ALTERNATIVE COOK, LLC™

happens. The recipe is the science part of this adventure in baking. It's your eyes, nose, sense of smell and touch that contribute to the "art" part of baking. With some practice, you'll develop a feel for the desired characteristics of the batter or dough or crust you are making.

FLOUR COMBINATIONS

I divide flours into three different categories – grain, protein and starch. If you're new to GFCF baking, refer back to the section, Stocking Your Pantry with Gluten-Free / Casein-Free Alternatives (Page 8), to reacquaint yourself with some of the workhouse flours of the GFCF kitchen. Through trial and error, I have concluded that the best ratio for most things (to start with) is 50% grain flour, 25% protein flour and 25% starch. If you'd rather omit the protein flour, substitute that with more grain flour. Avoid using only one type of grain flour in a recipe. It just doesn't work as well in gluten-free baking as a combination of two or more. My favorite combination is sorghum and brown rice flour. Some of the more exotic grains such as amaranth, teff, millet and quinoa should be used in smaller proportions in the recipes (25% or less) because they make the baked good "heavier" and/or impart a strong taste.

Protein flours are derived from beans or nuts. Bean flours can be substituted with other bean or legume flours. I usually limit bean flours to 25% because I like the result best with this proportion of flours. You may notice an off smell in the raw batter or dough when using bean flours. No worries; this bakes out and doesn't affect the final product. Nut meals can be substituted with seed meals, or omitted. I have found that with few exceptions, taking out the nut meal does not affect the final result.

Starches (except kudzu) are interchangeable in baked recipes. If your goal is to eat "whole" foods, arrowroot is considered whole.

If you are having a hard time finding the recommended ingredients, no problem. In most recipes, protein flours can be substituted with other protein (bean) flours, starches can be substituted with other starches, grain flours can be substituted with other grain flours and nut meals can be added or omitted with consistent results. Find more details on this in the Substitutions section (Page 20).

FATS

Fat is an integral part of any baked good, whether it is made with traditional or alternative ingredients. The recipes in this cookbook generally use oils such as walnut and sunflower, nut or seed butters, or margarine made from oil rather than saturated fats. Why? Because these oils are processed more efficiently in the body than are saturated fats. And the current consensus is that they are healthier for you. But, any oil can be used in place of the suggested oils, and any nut, seed or butter substitute can be used.

Store brands of margarine are often made from palm oil, and can even contain casein, a protein found in dairy products. If you are omitting casein from your diet and baking, you'll need to find an acceptable alternative. (Incidentally, many vegan or vegetarian "cheeses" also contain casein, so reading labels is paramount.) The "Margarine" recipe (Page 213) I developed, was created as a substitute for margarine in baking. It is made from oil, xanthan gum, citric acid and salt. It is simple to make in a food processor and works well in baked goods.

The American Heart Association (AHA) suggests that anyone over the age of two limit fat to 25-35% of total calories, and of that, saturated fats should be limited to 7%. The AHA suggests that fat sources should be primarily from nuts, seeds, fish and vegetable oils. We tend to think that saturated fats are those derived from animals. However, even though coconut and palm oil come from plants, they are highly saturated and should be used sparingly by those concerned about heart health.

GUMS

Gluten is what makes wheat bread have the lovely crumb it does, and contributes to the pleasing texture of most wheat-based baked goods. If you've ever seen pure gluten protein (called "seitan") being made, you've watched someone take a glob of wheat flour mixed with water, and agitate it under cold water until the starch falls away. What remains is a ball of gluten, which looks something like a ball of rubber bands. When making bread dough with wheat, these "rubber band strands" of gluten develop during the kneading process. The strands add tenderness and texture to the baked good.

If you tried the same process with gluten-free flour, the whole mass would disintegrate, since there's no gluten to hold it together. To compensate for the lack of these strands, we add gums and sometimes gelatins to our baked goods. Xanthan gum and guar gum are the most commonly used. Guar gum is usually added to the wet ingredients, and xanthan gum is added to the dry ingredients. A combination of both seems to work well in most recipes. The amount to use varies depending on the recipe – usually between ½ - 1 tsp. per cup of flour. The right amount may require some testing. And, some recipes do not call for any gum.

ACIDS

Acids are used in gluten-free baking for two reasons – to boost the leavening action and to balance the pH. Common acids include vinegar, lemon juice, ascorbic acid (vitamin C), citric acid, tomato juice, cocoa powder and cream of tartar.

PUTTING IT ALL TOGETHER / CONVERTING A RECIPE

I wrote most recipes starting with a blank sheet of paper, but have learned how to adapt traditional recipes along the way. Apparently all of that ratio analysis had some purpose! What follows is my "first-cut" approach – your general guideline to converting a recipe. Fine-tuning for perfection comes with testing. It all comes down to proportions of ingredients, acid, protein, gums and like-for-like substitutions. To adapt a recipe, follow these easy steps:

1. Start with a combination of flours in these ratios: 50% grain flour (brown rice or sorghum), 25% starch (cornstarch, tapioca or potato starch) and 25% protein flour (navy, fava, garbanzo, soy, gafava flour) or a different grain flour. One cup of wheat flour translates into ½ cup of grain flour, ¼ cup of bean flour and ¼ cup of starch.
2. Add 25-50% more leavening (baking powder, baking soda or yeast).
3. Add ½ to 1 tsp. acid (vinegar, citric acid, ascorbic acid dough enhancer, cream of tartar or citrus juice)
4. Add ½ tsp. of either xanthan gum to the dry ingredients or guar gum to the wet ingredients for every cup of flour or ¼ or each. For smaller baked items, you can omit gums.
5. Substitute butter with oil, and cow's milk with nut or rice milk (ideally with the same fat content).
6. Let the batter sit for a few minutes to absorb liquids before baking.

Sound easy? It really is, after you get the hang of it. Here is an example:

BROWNIES

Original Recipe	GFCF Adaptation
½ cup melted butter	½ cup sunflower oil
¾ cup sugar	¾ cup sugar
2 eggs	3 egg whites
1 tsp. vanilla	1 tsp. vanilla
	½ tsp. cider vinegar
	1 tsp. guar gum
⅓ cup cocoa powder	⅓ cup cocoa powder
½ cup flour	¼ cup sorghum flour
	2 TBS starch
	2 TBS protein flour
¼ tsp. baking powder	¼ plus ⅛ tsp. baking powder
1 tsp. coffee crystals	1 tsp. coffee crystals

Beat together the wet ingredients. Whisk together the dry ingredients and mix with wet ingredients. Divide into an oiled muffin pan and bake at 350° for 25 minutes.

Need more help? Or do you have a treasured or family-favorite recipe that you just can't get right using GFCF ingredients? We'll convert your recipe for you for a nominal fee. Go to **www.alternativecook.com** and click on "Convert a Recipe."

FOOD SUBSTITUTIONS

Substitutions can be a little daunting in the beginning but after a while they become one of the fun aspects of "playing" with a recipe and making it your own. Substitutions allow you to personalize a recipe to your own tastes, use ingredients you prefer and those you have on hand in your pantry.

There's really only one "rule" when substituting: consider the function an ingredient plays in the recipe. Is it a liquid, a binder, flour, starch or oil? Then substitute like-for-like, and in most cases, one-for-one. For example, if you want to substitute refined white sugar with something healthier, consider using one of the other granulated sugars. If you are substituting corn syrup (a sweetener) in a recipe, consider one of the other liquid sugars such as agave nectar or maple syrup. Substitutions are offered in many recipes, listed in order of my preference, based on our kitchen tests of making these recipes time and again. However, you can use any like-ingredient substitutions that suit you.

Unless otherwise noted, substitute ingredients in one-to-one proportions.

SUBSTITUTES FOR COW'S MILK

Nut or Seed Milk, made according to the recipe on Page 214.

Purchased rice, nut, or seed milk. For savory recipes, use "original" and for sweet recipes, use "vanilla."

Fruit juice or coffee – use as a liquid instead of milk in baked goods.

Flax milk – 1 TBS flax seed blended until smooth with 1 cup water.

Soy milk produces an unpleasant, acrid aroma when used in baked items, and is not my first choice as a substitute. But I do enjoy homemade yogurt made from soy milk!

SUBSTITUTES FOR WHEAT FLOUR

Rule of thumb: For one cup of wheat flour substitute 50% grain flour, 25% starch, and 25% protein flour in a recipe. It's not quite as simple as this, so please refer back to the section preceding this one, Converting a Recipe (Page 19), for additional information.

GLUTEN-FREE FLOUR SUBSTITUTIONS

Arrowroot – potato starch, cornstarch, tapioca flour, Expandex™

Amaranth flour – quinoa flour, millet flour, teff flour, brown rice flour

Buckwheat flour –Montina® flour or sorghum flour

Brown Rice flour – There's really no acceptable substitute for this flour; it is available online if you can't buy it locally.

Soy flour – any bean flour such as gafava, garbanzo, fava bean, white bean

Gafava flour – any bean flour such as soy, garbanzo, fava bean, white bean

Mesquite flour – brown rice flour

Montina® flour – substitute with another "grass family flour" such as buckwheat or sorghum

Teff flour – quinoa flour, amaranth flour, millet flour, brown rice flour

Quinoa flour – amaranth flour, millet flour, brown rice flour

Sorghum flour – There's really no acceptable substitute for this flour; it is available online if you can't buy it locally.

Sweet rice flour – arrowroot, cornstarch, potato starch, tapioca flour

White rice flour – brown rice flour (finely ground)

White bean flour – pinto bean, navy bean flour, white rice flour or white cornmeal (available in Mexican grocery stores)

STARCH SUBSTITUTIONS

Gluten-free baking often requires the use of starches. Most are interchangeable in a baked recipe. Starches are tapioca flour/tapioca starch, arrowroot, potato starch, cornstarch and Expandex™. Expandex™ really does make a difference in texture, resulting in a lighter product, so consider using it if it is available. (For an example of the difference, please see the **French Bread Comparison** on Page 153).

EGG SUBSTITUTES (FOR ONE EGG)

Flax mix – 1 TBS flax seed blended with ⅓ cup water until smooth.

Egg whites – use two egg whites per whole egg in a recipe.

Chia seeds – 2 tsp. of chia seeds mixed with ⅓ cup water. Let the chia seeds sit 10 minutes or so, until a "gel" forms. (This substitution does not need to be blended, but if you don't want little seeds in your baked item blend it before using.)

Ener-G® – egg replacement (use according to manufacturer's directions). This vegan substitution is made from starches and is used as a binder in recipes.

Soy protein isolate (use as described in the recipes).

Oil emulsified with liquid lecithin (use as described in the recipes).

A note on eggs: Some people are allergic to egg yolks, but not whites. Consider buying powdered egg whites (in the baking section of the grocery store, under the brand name Just Whites®) rather than buying eggs and throwing the yolks away. The powdered egg whites take a few minutes to reconstitute, so add the water, according to package directions, when you start your baked good and let them sit. Stir them until fully incorporated and use as you would an egg. Egg whites are pure protein and do not contain any cholesterol. Most recipes in this cookbook do not use whole eggs because of their high cholesterol content.

LIQUIDS

Water is the most common liquid used in cooking, and that is perfectly fine. However, there are times when your creative spirit wants expression, and a liquid substitute is one of the easiest ways to do this. Give zing to a white cake by using a tart fruit juice instead of water. Or use black tea or a deep, richly brewed coffee in a chocolate item for an added twist. Experiment and make recipes your own. It's the fun part of baking!

BUTTER SUBSTITUTES

"Margarine", made according to the recipe on Page 213.

Dairy-free, gluten-free butter substitutes. My preference is Spectrum Naturals® Spread from Spectrum Organic Products, Inc. This product is made with canola oil, tastes like butter and is free of saturated fat and cholesterol.

Oils (sunflower or walnut preferred for baked goods).

A combination of nut or seed butter mixed with oil and emulsified. Start with 50% nut butter, place into a mixer and thin with 50% oil. I've done this in recipes with beautiful results.

Mayonnaise or soy mayonnaise.

SUGAR SUBSTITUTES

Recipes in this cookbook use primarily natural sugars rather than highly refined or artificial sugars. Experiment with alternatives. For best results, if the original recipe calls for a granulated refined sugar, replace it with a granulated unrefined sugar such as maple or date sugar, organic cane sugar, or Sucanat®. Or, you can use ground freeze-dried fruits in place of granulated sugar to enrich baked goods.

Organic cane sugar can be substituted with:

Maple sugar (start with two-thirds as much sugar and add more to taste)

Date sugar (less sweet than sugar, may need to boost with other sweetener)

Brown sugar (not my preference, but could be used)

Florida Crystals®

ALTERNATIVE COOK, LLC™

Ground freeze-dried fruits (may need to boost with other sweetener)

Sucanat®

White sugar (not my preference, but could be used)

Xylitol

Stevia

I have discovered from doing the "ingredient comparisons" in this book that the crystal of sugar (whether organic cane sugar, maple sugar, Florida Crystals®, or Sucanat®) adds "bulk" to the recipe. If that is taken away, the baked good is less voluminous. Please refer to the photo of **Chocolate Dreams** on Page 123 for and example of this. If you are using a crystallized sugar and want to make the baked good sweeter, consider adding a tiny bit of stevia powder to the recipe. Since it lacks the crystal composition, it does not work by itself as a sweetener in a baked good, but does work well in puddings, custards and liquids, and to boost the sweetness of a batter.

Liquid sweeteners can be substituted with:

Agave nectar (start with half as much and add more to taste)

Concentrated fruit juice

Fruit puree or preserves (less sweet than sugar, may need to boost with other sweetener)

Honey

Molasses

Rice syrup (make sure it says gluten-free – some contain barley malt)

NUTS AND SEEDS

Raw nuts can be substituted with raw seeds and vice versa. Hemp seeds are the best seed substitution for nuts for the recipes in this cookbook. Other seeds can also be substituted for nuts, including raw sesame seeds and raw sunflower seeds. Substituting nuts for seeds and nuts for other nuts requires an "eye". For example, if a recipe calls for one almond, "eye" how much that would equate to in hemp seeds. I would substitute about ½ tsp. of hemp seeds per almond in a recipe. If the recipe calls for ½ cup chopped almonds, that is about the same as using the same amount of hemp seeds, because one hemp seed is about the same size as a piece of chopped almond.

TOFU AND SOY

If you are avoiding soy, use canned (salt-free) white beans in recipes calling for tofu. Rinse and drain them before using. Here again, use your "eye" to substitute. If a recipe called for ½ of a 16 oz. cake of tofu (i.e., 8 oz.), that would equate to one cup (8 oz.) of drained mashed (Great Northern or Cannellini or Navy) white beans.

OILS

Many of the recipes in this cookbook call for sunflower or walnut oil, or a non-dairy butter substitute made with canola oil - my three preferences for baking. Both the sunflower and walnut oil must be refined to withstand the baking temperatures. Use unrefined oils in salads and foods with low or no heat. If you prefer other oils, you could substitute any type of oil for recipes in this cookbook that have a high "smoke point." The "smoke point" of oil is the temperature that the oil begins to break down. Oils that can be used in baking with smoke points higher than 350°F include: canola, extra light olive oil (because it would not impart an olive taste), ghee (a type of clarified butter), grapeseed, hazelnut, refined peanut, corn, refined safflower, refined sunflower, or refined walnut. Coconut and/or palm oil are also possible substitutes. Here are the smoke points of these oils:

Oil	Smoke Point
Canola oil (Refined)	470°F
Coconut oil (Refined)	450°F
Ghee (clarified butter)	485°F
Grapeseed oil	420°F
Hazelnut oil	430°F
Olive oil (Extra light)	468°F
Palm oil	446°F
Peanut oil (Refined)	450°F
Corn oil (Refined)	450°F
Safflower oil (Refined)	510°F
Sunflower oil (Refined)	450°F
Walnut oil (Refined)	400°F

Changing the oils in a recipe is another way to "make it your own." For example, using ghee would impart a buttery flavor, coconut or palm oil would make foods more like the texture of traditional bakery-baked goods. I prefer the lightness of sunflower oil for light baked goods like cakes, and walnut oil for more dense baked goods like bars and cookies. When substituting oils, substitute one-for-one.

ESSENTIAL GFCF BAKING TIPS

My approach to baking GFCF was not always as relaxed and confident as it may seem in this book, on my DVDs, video streams, or website. Over the years there have been many failed loaves of bread and dozens upon dozens of cookies that crumbled at first bite, cakes of "goo" and baked goods that would work better as a paperweight. It's funny how some recipes just worked right from the start and others had to be tweaked many times to perfection. The **Yellow Cake** (Page 46) recipe alone took me about 20 trials to perfect. Iterations were all edible but the texture wasn't what I was after and since I don't ever want to throw away anything if I can help it, pie crust made from cake crumbs evolved from these trials. Sometimes the best innovations come from our failures. Bread has been another challenge, and rest assured, I have bread crumbs to use for months to come from developing the recipes in this book!

Baking GFCF is a journey of trial and error and even today I don't always turn out a perfect baked good the first time I develop a new recipe. So, take heart, and realize that with GFCF baking, patience, practice, taking good notes and having a sense of humor are the most important ingredients you'll bring to your epicurean adventures!

GENERAL GUIDELINES

* It's always a good idea to read through the entire recipe before beginning to make it to be sure you have all the ingredients.

* Assemble ingredients and baking equipment before you start making a recipe. Place two mixing bowls on the counter (one for the wet ingredients and one for dry), a whisk, rubber spatula, mixer, measuring cups and measuring spoons, and all your ingredients. Having these items out before you start saves time.

* GFCF baked goods often require multiple ingredients, and I used to dread having to drag out all of the ingredients to make something. Through testing this book, I developed the Tub Method. Make it easy and quick to assemble recipe ingredients by storing all your dry ingredients together in a tub in the refrigerator or freezer. The tub should contain your most frequently used ingredients: whole grain sorghum flour, whole grain brown rice flour, bean flours, leavenings, xanthan gum, guar gum, agar powder, starches, flax seeds, nuts and nut meals. When you are ready to bake, just place the tub on the counter and most of the dry ingredients you'll need are right at your fingertips. This saves a lot of time and keeps you from having to track down every ingredient for a recipe. It's also a handy at-a-glance way of noticing which items are getting low and need replenishing. Knowing that most everything I'll need to bake is in one centrally located tub motivates me to bake more often.

* Use the out-of-the-tub method to keep track of what ingredients you have used in the recipe. If the item is out-of-the-tub, it means it has already been measured into the recipe.

* Flours tend to settle as they sit, especially when the quantity is large. Before measuring, be sure to fluff the flour with the measuring cup.

* Measure dry ingredients with nested measuring cups. For example, use a separate ½ cup measure for ½ cup, and a ¼ cup measure for ¼ cup. Fluff flours, then dip the cup into the container (or spoon

flour lightly into the measuring cup) and level off with the dull side of a knife. Use the same technique in measuring dry ingredients with tablespoons or teaspoons; the measure should be level, not rounded. Measure wet ingredients in a measuring cup with a pouring spout.

* Measure oil before syrups/molasses/honey; it coats the measuring cup so the sticky ingredients slide right out.

* Do you add wet to dry or dry to wet? Generally, I recommend adding dry to wet to avoid wasting any of the wet ingredients. Sometimes though, when the wet ingredients are processed in a blender, I add the wet to the dry. Each recipe tells you what to do.

* Five Inch Rule. I've discovered that when using pans with less than a 5" diameter, gums are optional, but gums must be used when baking in pans with 5" or greater diameter.

* If you'd rather not use xanthan or guar gum, bake your item in several smaller pans, decreasing the baking time accordingly. In gluten-free baking, xanthan or guar gum are essential when baking larger (full-sized) goods.

* Ice a cooled cake (room temperature) with warm icing.

* Gluten-free batters are dry. Let them sit on the counter in the baking dish for a few minutes before putting them into the oven so they can absorb more moisture.

* Rather than rolling out dough on a lightly floured surface, try rolling gluten-free dough on an oiled surface. Oil your hands, the surface and the rolling pin for best results. The oil also helps brown the surface of your gluten-free baked good.

* Use spray-on oil or oil smeared with a paper towel to oil pans. "Clean" spray-on oils are available at the natural food store, just be sure they do not contain gluten (some are flour and oil combinations). Oil atomizers are available at cooking stores and could be used instead of purchased spray-on oils. Margarine does not work for oiling pans because of its high water content. Heavier oils like walnut work better for oiling pans than lighter oils like sunflower oil.

* Make meringues in a stainless steel or glass mixing bowl, but not in a plastic bowl. Meringue needs to grab hold of the surface to incorporate air.

* Before purchasing flours and grains – especially unusual grains that might not turn over quickly in the grocery store – check the package dates for freshness.

* Most families living a GFCF lifestyle have an investment in gluten-free grains and flours, so maximize their lifespan by storing them properly. Keep them in the freezer or refrigerator, not on the pantry shelf. Bring them to room temperature before baking. After opening, store them in air-tight containers, preferably glass. Most grains and flours last 3 months in the refrigerator and indefinitely in the freezer. Smell before using. If they smell rancid, discard them. (Believe me they will smell a lot worse when baked!)

* Most of the recipes in this cookbook are less sweet than their traditional counterparts. Recipes were tested with the ingredients listed. Reducing the sugar by up to ¼ cup should not impact the integrity of the recipe. Some people like to half the fat and add applesauce or mashed banana to compensate. I have not been successful doing this in most recipes. Rather, I would suggest making the recipes as listed, and savoring them in small portions over time.

OVEN

* Unless the recipe states differently, always bake items on the center rack of the oven. If you have two pans, place them side by side on the center rack, so they are not touching. If the oven isn't big enough for both pans, bake each pan separately.

* Oven temperatures vary, so consider purchasing an oven thermometer. Recipes were tested in standard (non-convection) ovens.

* If your oven has a hot spot, rotate the baked item halfway through the baking time.

* Baking times can vary depending on several factors: the type and size of your oven, and the humidity on the day you bake. While it's standard practice to keep an eye on the item baking, trust your nose! Start testing when you smell the heavenly aroma.

* Testing for doneness. With cakes, muffins, quick breads, brownies and bars, look for the item to pull away slightly from the sides of the pan, and spring back when lightly touched. Cookies should be slightly browned around the edges

* If the top of the baked good is sufficiently browned, but the item is not completely baked, just cover it with parchment paper and continue baking. Do not be afraid to bake an item covered in parchment 5-15 minutes longer in a medium-hot (350°) oven to get the right texture and moistness.

EGGS

* Reconstitute powdered egg whites with sparkling water for added "lift" in the baked good. A product called Just Whites® works really well and yolks aren't wasted. I've found they reconstitute faster by whisking the reconstitution water and any oil called for in the recipe. Dried eggs are pasteurized too, so you don't have to worry about bacteria commonly associated with eggs.

* All recipes calling for egg whites assume they have been reconstituted according to the manufacturer's instructions.

* If using eggs, assume the recipe calls for large eggs. One whole egg for every two egg whites can be substituted in most recipes (except in meringue-type recipes, where egg whites are the staple ingredient).

* To make egg whites stiffer, add 1 TBS finely ground organic cane sugar after they form peaks, then beat again until silky and stiff.

* Bring egg whites to room temperature before beating for maximum volume and best results.

LIQUID

* Use sparkling water instead of regular water in a recipe for a lighter baked good.

* If you are feeling creative, experiment with liquids – use herbal teas, coffee, fruit juice, melted frozen concentrated juices, vegetable juice, broths, liquors, etc. in recipes instead of the liquid called for. Just be sure to keep the measurement the same.

FLOURS

* All flours are not the same. Flour of the same type from one batch, manufacturer or part of the country may be dryer than from a different manufacturer, or region. Professional bakers weigh flours because of these variances. We non-professional bakers get a feel, through experience, of what the batter or dough should look like. Too thin? Add a little more flour. Too thick? Add more liquid (a tsp. at a time). Just be aware that these variances in flour moisture content exist and trust your judgment when making the recipe.

* Toasting flours can add a rich, nutty taste to a recipe. (Think of the taste difference between regular almonds and toasted almonds; it's a similar taste difference with flour.) Toasting amaranth or quinoa flour is especially good. Just place the flour in a dry saucepan over medium/high heat. Keep the flour moving until it becomes aromatic and turns golden brown. Cool and use in the recipe.

* Flours should be brought to room temperature before using. If you store your flours in the freezer, mix the recipe's dry ingredients together in a stainless steel bowl and put it on the stove burner, over low heat. Whisk the ingredients for a few minutes to warm the flours to room temperature. (Remember to set the bowl on a hot pad when adding the rest of the ingredients to avoid burning your countertop!)

BREAD

* Gluten-free yeast breads only rise once, so they take a lot less time to make than their gluten counterparts, which need two risings. Let the bread rise in the pan you plan to bake it in.

* Rising time depends on the temperature of your home, the altitude and the humidity in the air. For that reason, rising times are not given. Rather, let the bread rise until doubled in size, or until it reaches the top of the baking pan, as instructed in the recipe.

* Place parchment paper on top of the loaf halfway through baking, to avoid over-browning. It's typical for GF breads to bake 65-75 minutes – a little longer than their gluten-containing cousins.

* Though not necessary, an instant-read thermometer can help in baking GF breads. Since these breads use yeast, which is temperature sensitive, the thermometer can help you maintain the desired temperatures while mixing ingredients, and then later, to tell you when the loaf is done. Here's how to use the thermometer. When mixing the ingredients in the recipe, take the temperature of the dry ingredients (just stick the thermometer into the middle of the dry mix). Subtract that number from 140° and heat the liquid ingredients (once combined) to equal the difference. For example, if the dry ingredients are 65°, the wet ingredients should be 75°. The thermometer can also help tell you when the bread is done. The internal temperature of the bread should be between 205-207°. Instant or quick read thermometers are available at kitchen/cooking stores.

* Test yeast breads for doneness by using the old-fashioned method of removing a loaf from the baking pan and tapping the bottom with your fingertip. If it sounds hollow, the bread is likely done.

* Place the hot loaf on a rack and let it cool completely before cutting. The loaf is still baking while it cools. Cutting it before it is cool breaks the crust (seal) and lets out all of the steam. This can result in a gooier-than-desired product.

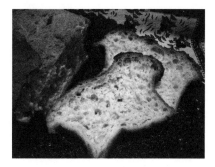

* If the bread has a thick crusty top, turn the loaf upside-down to cut smooth slices with a serrated knife.

* The recipes in this book use active dry yeast. Yeast needs to be activated before it can make your bread rise. This happens by combining it with warm water. Too cool, and the yeast doesn't come alive. Too hot and the yeast dies. Yeast "proofs" best in liquids between 105-110°. Add yeast to the warm water and wait about 5 minutes for it to foam (proof). If it doesn't proof, it means the yeast has died. Toss it out and try another packet. Check freshness dates on yeast packets before buying and using.

* Gluten-free breads are "batter" breads and use more liquids than the heavier, dough-ball consistency of wheat breads. Gluten-free bread batter resembles thick cake batter. The additional liquid can increase the baking time by 15-20 minutes.

* Gluten-free breads are not kneaded, because there is no gluten to develop – another time and energy saver for the baker!

* Although not tested this way, many of the yeast-bread recipes should work in a bread machine. Simply add the ingredients in the order specified for your machine, and be sure you have a machine with a "Gluten-free" setting – signifying that the bread will only rise one time before baking.

* When storing breads in the freezer, slice first and slip a piece of waxed paper between every slice to make it easy to remove slices later.

* You may notice in some recipes that offer both a small and a large loaf, the yeast measurement is not reduced proportionally for the small loaf. Yeast has diminishing returns – meaning that adding more to a recipe doesn't mean the loaf will rise more. The yeast measurements have been carefully calculated based on the loaf size.

BARS

* Bars freeze very well. Make a batch, divide into individual servings, place in plastic bags and freeze. Remove a bag, tuck it into your lunch box, backpack or purse and you'll have a sweet treat defrosted and ready at lunchtime or for a special afternoon snack.

* Bars have that dense, chewy goodness we all crave at times. This texture lends itself well to experimenting with ingredient substitutions, especially oils. Try walnut oil, or a half and half split of nut/seed butter and oil, emulsified with the whisk attachment or in a blender.

* Bake bars in an oiled glass or a dark metal pan for best results.

* Bars cut best once they've cooled. For those times when you just can't wait, warm your knife in hot water and dry it before each cut.

MUFFINS

✳ In traditional baking, we are advised to fill muffin cups two-thirds full. With gluten-free recipes, fill the muffin pans almost to the top with batter. This ensures beautiful baked goods.

✳ Fill empty muffin cups with ¼" of water before baking to even the pan and prevent empty muffin cups from burning, and to promote even-baking.

✳ Use paper muffin liners to prevent sticking and make for easy clean-up.

✳ It's not uncommon when using spray-on oiled muffin pans to get muffins with soggy bottoms. To avoid this, remove the muffins from the baking pan a few minutes after baking and let cool on a wire rack. The same goes for quick breads.

✳ I like to make larger-sized muffins, so I usually pour the batter into 9 or 10 of the muffin cups. If you prefer smaller muffins, simply distribute the batter into 12 pans and adjust the baking time accordingly.

COOKIES

✳ Baking cookies on a Silpat ensures non-stick, clean-edge perfection. Always use plastic (not metal) cooking utensils when using a Silpat, and do not use the Silpat as a cutting surface. If you do not have a Silpat, bake cookies on a lightly oiled non-stick surface.

✳ Let cookies sit on the baking sheet or Silpat 5 minutes after removing them from the oven to cool. They actually finish baking while they cool, so please be careful not to over-bake.

BROWNIES

✳ Brownies are always a hit at gatherings! If you plan to bring brownies to share, bake them in mini-muffin pans. This gives everyone a neat, individual serving.

✳ Have fun with brownie recipes! The recipes in this cookbook give you the basic brownie, so go ahead, experiment a little! Add different chopped dried fruits, nuts and/or chips. Chocolate brownies with chopped dried cherries – yum! Use liquid substitutes like coffee or herbal teas. Try extracts like peppermint (wonderful for holiday treats) or caramel (with a touch more salt) for an interesting twist.

✳ Brownies make delightful pie crusts! See the recipe for Ice Cream Pie on Page 204.

✳ You can never make brownies too often! Plus, they freeze well, so there's always one on hand for those 10 PM (or 10 AM) chocolate attacks!

✳ And while we're on the subject, measuring is really important in baking recipes, but if you are a little heavy handed with chocolate chips – well, that's OK!

ALTERNATIVE COOK, LLC™

PIES

✳ When a single crust pie recipe calls for the shell to be pre-baked, use pie weights to prevent the crust from rising from the bottom of the pan while baking. A handy and low-cost alternative is to use dried beans as weights. Once the beans are used they are no longer edible. Just store them in a glass jar as weights for future pies.

✳ Pies bake best in glass or dark metal pans.

✳ Roll out pie dough between two sheets of waxed paper or plastic wrap. Transfer one crust to the pan and simply peel off the paper. Easy!

✳ If the edges of the pie crust are browning too quickly, cover them with parchment paper.

✳ Experiment with different flours for crusts used with a savory filling. Try a toasted flour for a pie crust with a spinach or vegetable filling. Or add savory spices and herbs into the crust.

CRACKERS

✳ Dock crackers either by poking holes in them with a fork, or by rolling over them with a docking tool (available at kitchen stores). Docking is an important step in making crackers; the little holes make the crackers lighter and crisper.

✳ Transferring a rolled-out cracker onto a baking sheet ruins most of the shapes. It is best to roll out and cut on the baking surface and then peel away the excess dough.

CROSS CONTACT / CROSS CONTAMINATION

Even though I advocate "one meal the whole family will enjoy" it isn't likely that the whole household will become gluten-free if only one member of the family needs to eat that way. As a counselor at the Great Gluten Escape Camp in Gilmore, Texas, I have had the opportunity to meet many children who are eating a gluten-free and/or dairy-free diet. Many tell me that their parents fix a special meal for them – usually a meat, rice and a vegetable – and a different meal for the rest of the family. This saddens me, because cooking gluten and dairy free can be delicious (and transparent) for everyone. But gluten and dairy containing foods are advertised, popular and cheaper. So, if your kitchen is not completely gluten and dairy-free (and even mine isn't because my husband purchases ready-made wheat bread), you need to know some guidelines to avoid cross-contamination.

It's hard not to think some people border on paranoid and over-reacting when discussing cross-contamination. When first diagnosed, a rather high-strung dietitian told me never to use any appliance that had ever been used to make gluten-containing foods. I thought – wow! Not only are the ingredients expensive, but you are advocating that I buy a new bread machine, mixer, toaster oven, ovens, blender etc. This is thousands of dollars! So, I went home and gave away my beautiful Williams Sonoma bread machine and thoroughly cleaned my mixers and blenders. She specifically said to get a new GF toaster oven, and (still missing my bread machine) I thought cleaning the old toaster oven would be enough and proceeded to heat my GF cornbread muffin in it. About an hour later, I was as sick as if I had eaten a piece of wheat bread. She was right! Now we have two toaster ovens. If you live in a house with two large ovens, you could designate one for only gluten-free baking. Otherwise, oven bags are available to put your GF bread into and use in an oven also used for gluten.

When was the last time you slathered mustard on a piece of bread? And then stuck the knife back in the jar to get a little more? If the bread was made from wheat, barley or rye, the whole jar of mustard is now contaminated. Cross-contamination is so easy with condiments and jellies, it is best to just buy two of each and mark the lid of one as GF, and store it separate from the condiments used by gluten-eating family members. I have a Sharpie marker in my kitchen drawer for convenient GF marking and a designated shelf in the refrigerator.

Crumbs on the counter are also a problem. I ask guests to make their wheat bread sandwiches on paper towels to avoid cross-contamination. It is seemingly never ending, because if the crumbs get on the counter and you wipe them with a sponge, the sponge is contaminated and on and on. Potato chips are another problem. If someone is eating a wheat bread sandwich with their hands, and they reach into the bag of potato chips, the chips are now cross-contaminated. Scary isn't it? So, when I buy chips, I separate some into a plastic bag marked "GF", or take my serving out of the bag first. (This also keeps me from eating seconds and thirds of chips!)

Another problem is plastic utensils, such as the strainer for spaghetti. Since the plastic is porous, gluten can stick to that surface, even after being washed, and can cross-contaminate gluten-free foods. It is best to use stainless steel bowls and utensils. Baking pans should be separated because despite cleaning, crumbs

ALTERNATIVE COOK, LLC™

often stick in the corners and crevices and can easily cross-contaminate. If having two sets is too expensive or takes up too much room, consider making parchment liners or using paper muffin cups when baking gluten-free foods.

If you are working in a kitchen where someone has baked using flour containing gluten, the dust from the flour has likely cross-contaminated the kitchen. The kitchen should be washed; vents and filters should be cleaned.

It is really easy to cross-contaminate when measuring. I have a friend who is allergic to nuts. She could actually die if she is exposed to nuts. While testing this cookbook, I tried a lot of different nut meals and it was very common for me to dip the same measuring cup I used in the nut meal into one of the flours. I always wipe it with a towel first, but then the towel is cross-contaminated. Ideally, you would use one measuring cup for nut meals, and a different one for other items. Or you would wash and dry the measuring cup between measuring each item. Truth is, that is not likely to happen in most kitchens. I will not bake anything for her unless I start with all new unopened ingredients, clean utensils, scrubbed down kitchen and clean towels. The same goes for friends who usually cook with gluten in their kitchens and decide to make you a special gluten-free treat. It unfortunately is very likely that some of their baking ingredients are cross-contaminated.

Dairy cross-contamination is equally as common and usually happens with the serving spoon. People use the same serving spoon to serve something that might have a drop of dairy on it and then serve something that is supposed to be dairy-free. I've witnessed this at restaurants where guacamole is next to sour cream, and a drop of sour cream drips into the guacamole and is stirred in. Or, a server with a gloved hand who tops food with shredded lettuce then uses the same gloved hand to top the food with shredded cheese. You just can't be too careful.

You can easily see how one could become paranoid about all of this. So, what do we do? Well, paying attention is the first step. The second step is to try to understand your threshold. (Do you ever really know your threshold?) What might be tolerable for one person could put another in the hospital or worse. And what may have been tolerable to you in the past may cause reactions today. I've suspected for a while that the longer you are gluten or dairy free, the more sensitive you become over time.

Except for the toaster oven, cleaning my kitchen and appliances was enough. And, hopefully, this cookbook will equip you with the basics so you can cook for yourself or your family members following a special diet and avoid cross-contamination. In the meantime, take heart. Awareness in this country has increased dramatically in the past few years. Some restaurants that have gluten-free menus, have gluten-free stations in the kitchen and use different colored utensils and appliances for gluten-free food preparation. And considering it is estimated that only a small percentage of people with food intolerances are diagnosed, things will likely improve for us in time.

SAFE FOOD PRACTICES

I recently earned a certification from the National Restaurant Association for ServSafe – a course food-handlers around the world attend to ensure they know safe food practices. Although I have always been careful in my kitchen and thought I was practicing safe food handling, I learned a few things I'd like to share with you. Information from this section has been paraphrased from SafeServ Essentials, Fifth Edition, National Restaurant Association Education Foundation, 2008. Some of this is just good common sense, and some of it was eye-opening to me. The practices have been amended for the home-cook. Rules for handling food for the public are somewhat stricter than what is presented below.

The most common hazards to food safety are biological (pathogens), chemical (cleaners that get on foods), and physical (foreign objects). Pathogens include viruses, bacteria, parasites and fungi.

Pathogens can be minimized by:

✳ Washing hands thoroughly in warm water (100°F) before and during cooking

✳ Only cooking for others when feeling well

✳ Refrigerating food 41°F or lower

✳ Reheating food to 135°F or higher

✳ Cutting raw vegetables on a different cutting board than one used for raw meats

✳ Throwing away refrigerated foods after seven days

✳ Rotating foods – using first in, first out method to use oldest foods first

✳ Checking expiration dates and throwing away foods past the expiration date

✳ Using flours within twelve months of purchase if storing on the shelf

✳ Storing food in pantries at temperatures between 50°F and 70°F

✳ Storing foods in the refrigerator so raw meat juices do not drip on fresh vegetables

✳ Storing foods in clean, sanitized containers

✳ Washing hands after handling eggs, meat or fish

✳ Washing dishes in hot, soapy water (110°F)

✳ Purchasing foods from reputable stores

✳ Always washing fruits and vegetables before consuming

✳ Writing the date on foods before storing

* Cooking foods to their minimum internal temperature for 15 seconds: 165°F for poultry, meats; 155°F for ground meats, ground seafood; 145°F for seafood, steaks and eggs served immediately; 135°F for commercially processed ready-to-eat food, fruits, vegetables, grains, legumes that will be hot-held for serving.

* Storing cleaning products separate from food products

* Storing foods on a shelf at least 6" from the floor

* Storing all flours in a canister, washing and drying the canister before adding new flour. Never add new flour on top of old flour in a canister.

Safe practices to prevent pathogens:

* Pathogens can grow if food is at room temperature (between 41°F and 135°F, and most rapidly between 70°F to 125°F) for four hours. If food is held at this temperature for four or more hours, it must be thrown away.

* Wear clean clothes when cooking and tie hair back, bandage wounds (and cover with a single-use glove)

* If a food gets moldy, cut away at least one inch deeper from the mold before consuming or throw it away.

Chemical contamination can be minimized by:

* Removing all food items before cleaning surfaces used for food preparation

* Using "kitchen approved" cleaners

* Following the manufacturer's instructions

* Labeling all containers containing chemicals

Physical contamination can be minimized by:

* Looking at the food before you use it. Ensure no metal, paper, string, eggshells, fruit pits, nut shells, glass, etc. are in the foods you are using.

TIME AND MONEY SAVING TIPS

Can you think of anything better to invest in than your own, your child's, or your family's health and wellness? Few will dispute the sense and sensibility of following a GFCF diet if you are one of the hundreds of thousands of Americans for whom gluten and/or casein are health- or life-threatening ingredients.

Nevertheless when you venture away from corn, potatoes and rice (which is advisable when first diagnosed), living and eating GFCF can get pricey. Ingredients are generally more expensive than their gluten or casein filled alternatives. Depending on where you live, you may need to drive across town or to a nearby city to find a natural foods store or grocery store that stocks even the most common GFCF items. Even then, the selections are often limited. Buying online is an option, but to be even modestly economical, you need to buy in bulk, and pay shipping charges, which certainly do add up in the course of a year.

Even though I like to cook, a GFCF lifestyle can also be time-consuming. Not many of us are used to baking everything from scratch, and for some of you, doing so is an art you never learned in your mother's kitchen, as our society gets more and more entrenched in buying prepackaged mixes and wanting quick and easy meals.

Despite all of this, there are things you can do to save time and cut costs.

* Make your own dry mixes for baked goods, rather than purchasing pre-made mixes. This has several advantages. It is much cheaper, and you can use more wholesome, nutritional ingredients. The recipes in this cookbook are formatted to make it easy to do so. Assemble several batches of the "Dry" ingredients in one or more recipes, put in individual closable plastic bags, label with the recipe name and page number, and pop into the freezer. When it's time to bake, simply remove a bag, bring to room temperature, and combine with the remaining ingredients to finish the recipe.

* Bake an extra batch and freeze the rest. Use extra bread for bread crumbs, puddings, and croutons. Extra cake, muffins and cookies can be frozen and used for pie crusts or as a base for numerous recipes (as demonstrated in this cookbook). Granola is used in several recipes. Make a big batch and freeze it for quick use.

* Lots of store-bought special diet foods sit on the shelf a long time and are often dried-out or out-of-date by the time you purchase them. That's money down the drain. Some even contain preservative packets to extend their shelf life. Although they are great for travel, do you regularly want to eat a loaf of unfrozen bread that has an expiration date of six months or more on it?

* Set aside one day a week to bake. If you bake one or two things each Sunday and freeze some of each, you'll have a nice variety of baked goods for lunches, snacks, weekday or special occasion desserts, or to take to an impromptu evening gathering.

* Purchase more common ingredients at your local grocery store. For example, cornstarch, salt, juices, etc. are usually cheaper in the grocery store than at the natural food store. Visit an Asian, Mexican or Indian grocery store and stock up on ingredients you find there. Many carry unusual items that are staples of that culture's cuisine. And their prices are usually competitive.

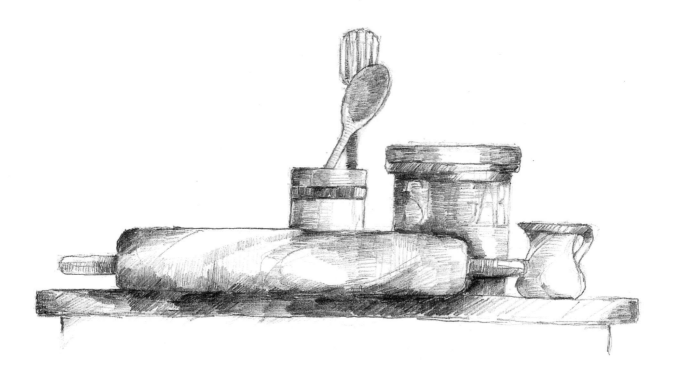

* Consider buying items you use most frequently, such as sorghum and brown rice flour, by the case or in bulk quantities to get added discounts.

* Make your own nut and seed meals. Both are very expensive to purchase pre-made, but are easy to make yourself. Simply put raw seeds or nuts into a food processor and blend. Make just as much as you need each time so the meals are fresh.

* Join (or start) a gluten-free group and purchase flours and other ingredients in bulk directly from the manufacturer. When the shipment arrives, have a festive gathering to divvy up the order, share recipes, etc. Some GF groups sell some of the harder-to-find, or expensive ingredients purchased in bulk as a fund-raiser.

* Gather 5-7 other people and create a GFCF cooking club. Once a week, each member cooks or bakes one item, in a large enough quantity for all other members. Club members gather together and trade foods. Presto – you have a week's worth of food.

* Pool your funds with your GFCF cooking club and buy seldom used appliances such as bread machines, waffle makers, tortilla presses, yogurt makers and dehydrators to share.

Cakes and Cupcakes

A lovely, decorated cake is the centerpiece of most festive occasions. Whether it is a delicate lady finger cake, a homey applesauce cake or a kid-friendly birthday cake, there are plenty of great tasting options!

Red Velvet Cake with White Icing, 40

Lemon Chiffon Cake with Marshmallow Cream Icing, 42

Almond Apricot Bundt Cake with Apricot Glaze, 44

Yellow Layered Cake with Raspberry Filling and Chocolate Tahini Icing, 46

Applesauce Cake with "Cream Cheese" Frosting, 48

"Cheesecake" with Glazed Strawberries, 50

Flourless Chocolate Cake, 52

Luscious Lemon Lady Finger Cake, 53

Angel Food Cake, 54

Chocolate, Chocolate Chip Angel Food Cake, 55

Lemon Angel Food Cake with Lemon Cream Icing, 56

"Devilish" Chocolate Layered Cake with Marshmallow Filling
and Chocolate Avocado Icing, 58

Baked Alaska with Meringue Icing, 60

Strawberry Cupcakes with Cashew Cream Icing, 62

Orange Cupcakes with Orange Icing, 64

Lemon Bliss Cupcakes with Lemon Glaze, 66

RED VELVET CAKE WITH WHITE ICING

RED VELVET CAKE

My aunt was famous for her Red Velvet cakes. They were the decadent, rich delight we all anxiously awaited after her glorious spiced shrimp dinners. This conversion of her famous recipe will capture your equal applause.

Dry Ingredients

1 cup whole grain sorghum flour

¾ cup arrowroot or sweet rice flour

½ cup tapioca flour

¼ cup cornstarch or potato starch

3 TBS cocoa powder

1 tsp. xanthan gum

1 tsp. baking soda

1 tsp. baking powder

½ tsp. salt

A few drops of natural red food coloring OR 1 TBS beet powder (optional)

Wet Ingredients

6 egg whites

1 cup rice, nut or seed milk

¾ cup walnut or sunflower oil

1½ cups organic cane sugar

1 tsp. guar gum

2 tsp. vanilla

2 tsp. rice vinegar

PREHEAT OVEN TO 325°F.

1. In a separate bowl whisk dry ingredients together.

2. Beat egg whites in a mixer with the paddle attachment until soft peaks form. Add other wet ingredients. Beat 1 minute on high speed. Add dry ingredients. Beat until incorporated. Let batter rest a few minutes.

3. Pour batter into two round 8" floured pans. Bake 40-45 minutes. Turn out on a rack to cool. Ice cake with **White Icing** (Page 41).

Nutritional Information Per Serving
Servings 12 ✳ Calories 246 ✳ Fat 14g ✳
Protein 4g ✳ Carbohydrates 26g ✳ Cholesterol 0mg ✳
Sodium 115mg ✳ Fiber 1g

ALTERNATIVE COOK, LLC™

WHITE ICING

A simple white icing is a staple for every baker's repertoire. This creamy, light and delicious frosting can be used on all sorts of cakes and baked goodies.

Ingredients
½ cup butter substitute
4 TBS powdered rice or soy milk
5 TBS liquid rice, nut or seed milk
2 tsp. vanilla
1 lb. box confectioner's sugar
1 TBS butter flavor extract (optional)

1. Stir butter substitute, powdered milk and rice, nut or seed milk in a saucepan until dissolved. Turn on heat to high and bring to a boil, stirring constantly.

2. Remove from heat and beat in vanilla, confectioner's sugar and butter flavor.

3. Spread on cooled cake while icing is warm.

Nutritional Information Per Serving
Servings 12 ✳ Calories 230 ✳ Fat 2g . Protein 0g ✳
Carbohydrates 42g ✳ Cholesterol 0mg ✳
Sodium 130mg ✳ Fiber 0g

LEMON CHIFFON CAKE
WITH MARSHMALLOW CREAM ICING

LEMON CHIFFON CAKE

Impress your family or guests with a slice of this luscious, lemony sensation. They'll be even more excited to learn this delicious cake is less fattening than its buttery-based traditional counterparts. Try it for a fabulous fancy birthday cake.

Dry Ingredients

¼ cup whole grain sorghum flour

¼ cup whole grain brown rice flour

½ cup tapioca flour

½ cup sweet rice flour or arrowroot

½ cup cornstarch

2¾ tsp. baking powder

1 tsp. xanthan gum

½ tsp. salt

4 drops turmeric-based food coloring (optional)

Wet Ingredients

¼ cup walnut oil

¼ cup sunflower oil

1 tsp. lecithin

½ cup sparkling water

¼ cup lemon juice

2 tsp. vanilla

1 cup organic cane sugar

1 tsp. guar gum

1 tsp. lemon oil (or a few drops, depending on the taste and oil pungency)

1 TBS freshly grated lemon zest

Egg Whites

1 cup egg whites (about 8-10 egg whites)

½ tsp. cream of tartar

PREHEAT OVEN TO 325°F.

1. Whisk dry ingredients together. In a mixer, combine oils and lecithin. Beat 2 minutes until creamy. Add the remaining wet ingredients. Emulsify by beating 4-5 minutes. Add dry ingredients. Beat until smooth. Set aside.

2. In a separate bowl, beat egg whites and cream of tartar until stiff. Add one-third of the egg whites to the cake batter to thin. Then fold the batter into the remaining egg whites, in thirds, barely incorporating.

3. Place in a 10" angel food cake pan and bake 45 minutes. Cover with parchment paper and bake 40-45 more minutes. (Total baking time 1 hour and 25-30 minutes.) Remove from oven and leave in pan until cake cools. Run a knife around the edges to loosen sides and remove from pan. (Do not invert to cool.) Frost with **Marshmallow Cream Icing** (Page 43) and decorate.

> **Nutritional Information Per Serving**
> Servings 12 ✳ Calories 249 ✳ Fat 10g ✳
> Protein 3g ✳ Carbohydrates 37g ✳ Cholesterol 0mg ✳
> Sodium 128mg ✳ Fiber 1g

MARSHMALLOW CREAM ICING

Frost the Lemon Chiffon Cake with this icing, then decorate with sprinkles, grated lemon rind, nuts, or chocolate shavings. Be creative! This heavenly icing can make anything elegant.

Ingredients
2 egg whites
1 cup organic cane sugar
¼ tsp. cream of tartar
3 TBS cold water
3 TBS lemon juice
1 tsp. vanilla
Tiny pinch of salt

1. Place all ingredients except vanilla into a double boiler. Using a hand-held mixer, beat on low speed for 3 minutes or until water boils and sugar is melted.

2. Reduce the heat and beat 7 minutes on high speed until it thickens to the consistency of marshmallow cream. Add vanilla and mix until incorporated.

3. Ice cooled cake.

Nutritional Information Per Serving
Servings 12 ✳ Calories 58 ✳ Fat 0g . Protein 1g ✳
Carbohydrates 17g ✳ Cholesterol 0mg ✳
Sodium 10mg ✳ Fiber 0g

ALMOND APRICOT BUNDT CAKE WITH APRICOT GLAZE

ALMOND APRICOT BUNDT CAKE

This moist, elegant cake is a wonderful addition to a brunch. It is a hit with the non-gluten-free crowd too! I prefer the taste of unsulphured dried apricots over the sulphured kind.

Wet Ingredients

½ cup chopped dried apricots

6 egg whites

1 cup sunflower or walnut oil

1 tsp. liquid lecithin (optional)

¾ cup rice, nut or seed milk

1½ cups organic cane sugar

1 tsp. guar gum

1 tsp. almond extract

2 tsp. vanilla

1 tsp. apple cider vinegar

Dry Ingredients

1 cup whole grain sorghum flour

½ cup whole grain brown rice flour

½ cup almond meal

½ cup sweet rice flour or cornstarch

½ cup white bean, garbanzo, gafava or soy flour

2 tsp. baking powder

1 tsp. xanthan gum

½ tsp. salt

¾ cup toasted slivered almonds (reserve ¼ cup)

PREHEAT OVEN TO 350°F.

1. Boil chopped apricots in water until soft. Drain, dry and set aside.

2. In a mixer, whip egg whites until soft peaks form, then add the remaining wet ingredients and mix well.

3. In a separate bowl, whisk dry ingredients together. (Reserve ¼ cup toasted slivered almonds for decoration.)

4. Combine dry ingredients with wet ingredients and mix on low speed until incorporated.

5. Spray a 10 x 4" Bundt cake pan with spray-on oil. Place reserved ¼ cup of slivered almonds in the bottom of the cake pan. Pour batter into the pan (over the nuts). Bake 60 minutes, covering with parchment after 30 minutes to prevent over-browning. Cool. Turn out on a serving plate. Glaze with **Apricot Glaze** (Page 45), or sprinkle with confectioner's sugar.

Nutritional Information Per Serving
Servings 16 ✳ Calories 355 ✳ Fat 19g ✳
Protein 7g ✳ Carbohydrates 42g ✳ Cholesterol 0mg ✳
Sodium 28mg ✳ Fiber 2g

APRICOT GLAZE

This ever-so-easy glaze adds a beautiful glossy finish to your Almond Apricot cake.

Ingredients
½ jar apricot 100% fruit spread
¼ cup apricot juice or apple juice

1. Combine fruit spread and juice in a saucepan and cook on medium heat until it thickens.

2. Poke holes in the cake with a fork and pour glaze on top.

Nutritional Information Per Serving
Servings 16 ✳ Calories 26 ✳ Fat 0g ✳ Protein 0g ✳
Carbohydrates 7g ✳ Cholesterol 0mg ✳
Sodium 4mg ✳ Fiber 0g

YELLOW LAYERED CAKE WITH RASPBERRY FILLING AND CHOCOLATE TAHINI ICING

YELLOW LAYERED CAKE WITH RASPBERRY FILLING

Purchased fruit-only raspberry preserves are a lovely compliment to the flavorful yellow cake and the heavenly chocolate icing. It's a quick and easy filling. Experiment with other fruit preserves for a variation on this cake.

Wet Ingredients

4 egg whites

½ cup butter substitute

1 tsp. liquid lecithin

2 tsp. vanilla

1 cup rice, nut or seed milk

¾ cup sparkling water

1 cup organic cane sugar

1 tsp. rice vinegar

Dry Ingredients

½ cup whole grain sorghum flour

½ cup garbanzo, gafava or soy bean flour

¼ cup whole grain brown rice flour

1 cup cornstarch

½ cup tapioca flour

½ tsp. xanthan gum

2 tsp. baking soda

1 tsp. baking powder

½ tsp. salt

1 10 oz. jar fruit-only raspberry preserves

PREHEAT OVEN TO 350°F.

1. In a mixer with the whisk attachment, beat egg whites until foamy. Beat in each wet ingredient separately until mixture is emulsified. Beat several minutes on medium speed. This adds "lift" to the cake.

2. In a separate bowl, whisk dry ingredients together. Add to wet ingredients, and mix together on low speed until incorporated (about 1 minute).

3. Line the bottom of two 9" round pans with parchment paper. Spray with spray-on oil and lightly dust with sorghum flour. Place batter in pans and bake 35-45 minutes (until cake springs back to the touch and pulls away from the sides). Place parchment paper over the tops of the cakes after 25 minutes to prevent over-browning. Turn out on a rack to cool.

4. Fill the layers with fruit-only raspberry preserves. Frost top and sides with **Chocolate Tahini Icing** (Page 47).

Nutritional Information Per Serving
Servings 12 ✳ Calories 263 ✳ Fat 9g ✳ Protein 3g ✳
Carbohydrates 42g ✳ Cholesterol 0mg ✳
Sodium 446mg ✳ Fiber 1g

CHOCOLATE TAHINI ICING

This is my favorite chocolate icing and another good staple for your recipe box.
There's something extra-special about the combination of chocolate, sesame
and maple. Mmmm.

Ingredients

1 cup maple syrup

1¼ cups raw tahini

½ cup cocoa powder

1. In a saucepan, heat the maple syrup just to the boiling point. Remove from heat and whisk in tahini and cocoa powder. Beat until fully blended and smooth.

2. Frost cooled cake while icing is warm.

Nutritional Information Per Serving

Servings 12 ✳ Calories 218 ✳ Fat 13g ✳ Protein 4g ✳
Carbohydrates 23g ✳ Cholesterol 0mg ✳
Sodium 31mg ✳ Fiber 2g

APPLESAUCE CAKE WITH "CREAM CHEESE" FROSTING

APPLESAUCE CAKE

A friend and I were asked to bring cakes to a meeting, so we decided to "duel" our best applesauce cakes. She made her traditional recipe with wheat flour and dairy products, and I made this GFCF conversion. We served small pieces side-by-side on the plate to 25 women. They could not tell the difference and loved both! Another testament that "baking without" can still be just as delicious!

Wet Ingredients

2½ cups applesauce, unsweetened

½ cup apple juice

½ cup walnut oil

4 egg whites

1 tsp. apple cider vinegar

Dry ingredients

1¼ cups whole grain sorghum flour

½ cup whole grain brown rice flour

½ cup whole grain teff flour

¼ cup cornstarch or arrowroot

1 cup Sucanat®

½ cup organic cane sugar

2 tsp. xanthan gum

1½ tsp. baking soda

1½ tsp. salt

¾ tsp. baking powder

2 tsp. cinnamon

½ tsp. cloves

½ tsp. allspice

PREHEAT OVEN TO 350°F.

1. Mix wet ingredients with a hand mixer. Whisk dry ingredients together separately. Add to wet ingredients. Mix until incorporated, scraping sides occasionally.

2. Pour into an oiled 13 x 9 x 2" pan. Let batter sit for 10 minutes. Bake 60-65 minutes. (For cupcakes, place batter in an oiled cupcake pan and bake 25-30 minutes.)

3. Ice with **"Cream Cheese" Frosting** (Page 49).

Nutritional Information Per Serving

Servings 12 ✳ Calories 259 ✳ Fat 10g ✳ Protein 4g ✳ Carbohydrates 39g ✳ Cholesterol 0mg ✳ Sodium 210mg ✳ Fiber 2g

"CREAM CHEESE" FROSTING

Tasters loved the Applesauce Cake but ooh'd and aah'd about the icing.

Ingredients
⅓ lb. extra soft tofu
2 tsp. lemon juice
1 TBS walnut oil
Tiny pinch of salt
1 tsp. nutritional yeast
1 tsp. vanilla
4 - 4½ cups confectioner's sugar
1 tsp. butter flavor (optional)

1. Place tofu in a steamer and steam for 10 minutes. Press tofu between layers of paper towels to remove moisture.

2. Place ingredients, except confectioner's sugar, in a food processor and process until smooth. Add confectioner's sugar, pulsing until desired frosting consistency is achieved.

Nutritional Information Per Serving
Servings 12 ✳ Calories 185 ✳ Fat 2g ✳ Protein 2g ✳
Carbohydrates 41g ✳ Cholesterol 0mg ✳
Sodium 2mg ✳ Fiber 0g

"CHEESECAKE"
WITH GLAZED STRAWBERRIES

"CHEESECAKE"

This creamy, sensuous treat is sure to be a hit with your cheesecake lovers!
Serve plain or with fresh or glazed berries.

Ingredients

1 lb. extra soft tofu

1 TBS lemon juice

1 TBS freshly grated lemon peel
(or ½ tsp. dried)

1 TBS apple cider vinegar

¼ cup walnut oil

2 tsp. nutritional yeast

½ cup finely ground organic cane sugar

4 egg whites

2 tsp. vanilla

2 tsp. cornstarch

Pinch salt

1 recipe **Lemon "Zesties" Pie Crust**
(Page 208)

PREHEAT OVEN TO 350°F.

1. Press tofu between layers of paper towels to remove moisture.

2. Place tofu and remaining cheesecake ingredients in a food processor and process until smooth.

3. Spoon into a pre-baked **Lemon "Zesties" Pie Crust** made in an 8½ x 1½" pie pan, or four individual 4 x ½" pie pans. Bake 40-45 minutes.

4. Cool in refrigerator for 2 hours and serve with fresh or **Glazed Strawberries** (Page 51).

Nutritional Information Per Serving
Servings 8 ✳ Calories 184 ✳ Fat 10g ✳
Protein 8g ✳ Carbohydrates 16g ✳ Cholesterol 0mg ✳
Sodium 32mg ✳ Fiber 2g

GLAZED STRAWBERRIES

These make a beautiful, fruity topping for the "Cheesecake", or can be used as a pie filling.

Ingredients

1 cup whole fresh strawberries

½ cup apple juice concentrate

2 TBS organic cane sugar

2 TBS arrowroot or cornstarch

½ tsp. beet powder or a few drops of natural red food coloring (optional)

1. Slice the strawberries. Set aside.

2. Combine apple juice, sugar and arrowroot in a saucepan on high heat. Whisk until thickened, remove from heat and add strawberries. Cool. Pour over chilled cheesecake slices before serving.

Nutritional Information Per Serving

Servings 8 ✳ Calories 50 ✳ Fat 0g ✳ Protein 0g ✳
Carbohydrates 12g ✳ Cholesterol 0mg ✳
Sodium 1mg ✳ Fiber 1g

FLOURLESS CHOCOLATE CAKE

The texture and taste of this cake is just heavenly, and it is equally as rich and decadent as its dairy-containing counterparts! This recipe uses a rich macadamia nut cream, but you could substitute any raw nut or seed. Using a spring form pan ensures success.

Cream
½ cup unsalted dry-roasted or raw macadamia nuts
½ cup water

Ingredients
4 eggs, separated
½ cup semi-sweet GFCF chocolate chips
½ cup organic cane sugar
1 tsp. vanilla
Pinch salt

Nutritional Information Per Serving
Servings 6 ✳ Calories 281 ✳
Fat 17g ✳ Protein 6g ✳
Carbohydrates 30g ✳
Cholesterol 141mg ✳
Sodium 49mg ✳ Fiber 2g

PREHEAT OVEN TO 350°F.

1. Prepare four, 4 x 1¾" spring form pans by cutting parchment paper rounds the size of the bottom of the pan, and spraying the paper and pan sides with spray oil and coating with sugar.

2. Make cream by blending nuts and water in a blender a few minutes until completely smooth.

3. Place chocolate chips in a bowl and microwave until melted, stirring occasionally. Add Cream and whisk until incorporated. Set aside.

4. Whip egg yolks with half of the sugar until yolks are lemony yellow. Add yolk mixture to cooled chocolate mixture. Add vanilla.

5. Beat egg whites with the other half of the sugar until stiff peaks form. Fold chocolate mixture into egg whites – being careful not to let them fall.

6. Place mixture into prepared pans. Gently smooth the top, and run your finger around the edges to clean. Bake 40-45 minutes. Place parchment over top after 20 minutes to prevent over-browning. Remove from oven and cool in pans 20 minutes. Run a knife around the edges and "spring" the cake from the pan. Cool in refrigerator for 2-3 hours. Serve garnished with fresh raspberries.

ALTERNATIVE COOK, LLC™

LUSCIOUS LEMON LADY FINGER CAKE

A silky smooth lemon filling encased by light, crisp Lady Fingers. This cake has a lovely balance of tart and sweetness, and I think you'll be delighted with how nuts or seeds make such a rich, creamy filling.

Ingredients

1 cup warm water

2 tsp. agar powder

1 cup raw almonds
 OR ¾ cup raw hemp seeds

½ cup lemon juice

2 TBS lemon zest
 OR 1 tsp. dried lemon peel

½ cup Limoncello (lemon liquor or more lemon juice)

1 tsp. lemon oil (or a few drops, depending on the taste and oil pungency)

½ cup agave nectar

1 tsp. vanilla

1 TBS kudzu

1. Boil raw almonds for 1 minute. Pop off skins. Dry. If using hemp seeds, measure and add to blender.

2. In a blender, combine all of the ingredients and process until smooth. This may take 3-4 minutes. Strain mixture into a pot. Heat on high heat while whisking constantly until mixture thickens and coats the back of a spoon.

3. Line the bottom and sides of a 9" round spring-form pan with whole **Lady Fingers** (Page 98). Pour lemon filling into pan. Chill cake 3 hours before serving.

Nutritional Information Per Serving
Servings 8 ✳ Calories 175 ✳ Fat 10g ✳ Protein 4g ✳
Carbohydrates 22g ✳ Cholesterol 0mg ✳
Sodium 29mg ✳ Fiber 1g

ANGEL FOOD CAKE

Such a heavenly cake! Light and delicious, Angel Food Cake is a perfect companion to many different flavor accents, from rich chocolate syrup to peak-of-the-season fresh fruit or berries. It's even good plain, eaten right out of the hand! This recipe uses sparkling water to reconstitute the powered egg whites, adding "lift" to the cake.

Wet Ingredients

½ cup Just Whites® dried egg whites reconstituted with
1½ cups sparkling water
OR 12 egg whites
⅔ cup organic cane sugar
1 tsp. cream of tartar
1 tsp. vanilla

Dry Ingredients

½ cup whole grain sorghum flour
¼ cup white bean, navy or pinto bean flour
¼ cup cornstarch, tapioca flour, arrowroot, potato starch or Expandex™
⅔ cup organic cane sugar or Florida Crystals®
1 tsp. xanthan gum
Pinch salt

PREHEAT OVEN TO 375°F.

1. With the whisk attachment, beat the egg whites until foamy. Add cream of tartar then sugar, one TBS at a time, until stiff peaks form. Add vanilla.

2. In a separate bowl, sift the dry ingredients together. Gently fold dry ingredients into egg white mixture by hand to keep "lift" and air in the batter.

3. Place mixture in a clean, 10" dry tube pan. Bake 40-45 minutes. Cover with parchment paper after baking 30 minutes to prevent over-browning. Remove from oven and invert pan until cool. Run a knife around the edges and the center tube to release cake from the pan. Drizzle with chocolate syrup and serve with fresh berries.

Nutritional Information Per Serving
Servings 12 ✳ Calories 144 ✳ Fat 1g ✳ Protein 5g ✳
Carbohydrates 31g ✳ Cholesterol 0mg ✳
Sodium 56mg ✳ Fiber 0g

CHOCOLATE, CHOCOLATE CHIP ANGEL CAKE

This is a dream-come-true delectable: a fat-free* chocolate cake with lots of protein! This was a favorite among my testers and tasters, not to mention friends and family! Pop a few slices in the freezer for a quick snack.

Wet Ingredients

½ cup Just Whites® dried egg whites reconstituted with
1½ cups sparkling water
 OR 12 egg whites
⅔ cup organic cane sugar
1 tsp. cream of tartar
1 tsp. vanilla

Dry Ingredients

½ cup whole grain sorghum flour
¼ cup cocoa powder
¼ cup cornstarch, tapioca flour, arrowroot, potato starch or Expandex™
⅔ cup organic cane sugar or Florida Crystals®
1 tsp. xanthan gum
Pinch salt
½ cup GFCF chocolate chips (*optional; adds fat to the recipe)

PREHEAT OVEN TO 375°F.

1. With the whisk attachment, beat egg whites until foamy. Add cream of tartar then sugar, one TBS at a time until stiff peaks form. Add vanilla.

2. In a separate bowl, sift together the dry ingredients. Fold dry ingredients into egg white mixture barely incorporating. (Marbling is good.)

3. Place in a clean, dry 10" tube pan. Bake 40-45 minutes. Cover with parchment after baking 30 minutes to prevent over-browning. Remove from oven and invert pan until cool. With a serrated knife, cut around the edges and the center tube to release cake from the pan.

Nutritional Information Per Serving

Without Chocolate Chips:
Servings 12 ✳ Calories 143 ✳ Fat 0g ✳ Protein 4g ✳ Carbohydrates 31g ✳ Cholesterol 0mg ✳ Sodium 56mg ✳ Fiber 1g

With Chocolate Chips:
Servings 12 ✳ Calories 185 ✳ Fat 3g ✳ Protein 5g ✳ Carbohydrates 37g ✳ Cholesterol 0mg ✳ Sodium 58mg ✳ Fiber 1g

LEMON ANGEL CAKE
WITH LEMON CREAM ICING

LEMON ANGEL CAKE

Pair the light, airy quality of an angel food cake with the freshness of lemon to create a special, yet not too-filling cake. This is a perfect dessert for a summer gathering.

Wet Ingredients

½ cup Just Whites® dried egg whites
reconstituted with
1 cup sparkling water
 OR 12 egg whites
½ cup lemon juice
⅔ cup organic cane sugar
1 tsp. cream of tartar
1 tsp. vanilla

Dry Ingredients

½ cup whole grain sorghum flour
¼ cup navy or pinto bean flour
¼ cup cornstarch, tapioca flour,
arrowroot, potato starch or Expandex™
⅔ cup organic cane sugar
1 tsp. xanthan gum
1 tsp. fresh lemon zest
Pinch salt

PREHEAT OVEN TO 375°F.

1. In a mixer, beat the egg whites until foamy. Add cream of tartar then sugar, one TBS at a time until stiff peaks form. Add vanilla.

2. In a separate bowl, sift the dry ingredients together. Manually fold dry ingredients into wet, barely incorporating.

3. Place in a clean, 10" dry tube pan. Bake 40-45 minutes. Cover with parchment paper after 30 minutes to prevent over-browning. Remove cake from oven and invert pan until cool. Run a knife around the edges and the center tube to release cake from pan.

4. Cool completely and frost with **Lemon Cream Icing** (Page 57) or sprinkle with confectioner's sugar and decorate with fresh strawberries.

Nutritional Information Per Serving
Servings 12 ✳ Calories 171 ✳ Fat 1g ✳
Protein 10g ✳ Carbohydrates 32g ✳ Cholesterol 0mg ✳
Sodium 134mg ✳ Fiber 1g

LEMON CREAM ICING

Easy, delicious and refreshing. You'll use it often!

Ingredients

¼ cup warm water

2 tsp. agar powder

¾ cup raw cashews or hemp seeds

½ cup water

½ cup lemon juice

1 tsp. lemon oil (or a few drops, depending on the taste and oil pungency)

½ cup agave nectar

1 tsp. vanilla

1 TBS kudzu

1. Dissolve agar powder in warm water.

2. Combine all ingredients (including agar powder and water mixture) in a blender and process until mixed together.

3. Pour into a saucepan and heat over high heat until thick mixture thickens, stirring constantly. Ice cooled cake. Refrigerate 2 hours before serving.

Nutritional Information Per Serving
Servings 12 ✳ Calories 125 ✳ Fat 7g ✳ Protein 3g ✳
Carbohydrates 15g ✳ Cholesterol 0mg ✳
Sodium 18mg ✳ Fiber 1g

"DEVILISH" CHOCOLATE LAYERED CAKE WITH MARSHMALLOW FILLING AND CHOCOLATE AVOCADO ICING

"DEVILISH" CHOCOLATE LAYERED CAKE

This is a perfect birthday cake – chocolate cake, marshmallow filling and even a surprise – icing made from avocados! Trust me, it is fantastic! I served this to our friends at my husband's "significant" birthday party. Friends are still talking about that cake! And it freezes well (not that there will be any left to freeze).

Wet Ingredients
4 egg whites
½ cup butter substitute
1 tsp. liquid lecithin
2 tsp. vanilla
1 cup rice, nut or seed milk
¾ cup sparkling water
1 cup organic cane sugar
1 tsp. rice vinegar

Dry Ingredients
½ cup whole grain sorghum flour
¼ cup whole grain brown rice flour
½ cup cocoa powder
1 cup arrowroot
½ cup white rice flour
½ tsp. xanthan gum
2 tsp. baking soda
1 tsp. baking powder
½ tsp. salt

1 (7 oz.) jar purchased marshmallow cream (for filling)

PREHEAT OVEN TO 350°F.

1. In a mixer, beat egg whites until foamy. Beat in each additional wet ingredient separately until mixture is emulsified. Beat an additional 3-4 minutes.

2. In a separate bowl, whisk dry ingredients together. Add to wet ingredients, and mix together on low speed until blended.

3. Line two 9" round pans with parchment paper. Spray with spray-on oil and lightly dust with sorghum flour. Place batter in pans and bake 35-45 minutes (until cake springs back to the touch and pulls away from the sides). Place parchment paper over the tops of the cakes after 25 minutes to prevent over-browning. Turn out on a rack to cool.

4. Fill the layers with purchased marshmallow cream. Frost top and sides with **Chocolate Avocado Icing** (Page 59).

Nutritional Information Per Serving
Servings 12 ✳ Calories 257 ✳ Fat 9g ✳ Protein 3g ✳
Carbohydrates 43g ✳ Cholesterol 0mg ✳
Sodium 455mg ✳ Fiber 2g

CHOCOLATE AVOCADO ICING

You won't believe how good this is — and EASY! Who would have thought avocado and chocolate would marry so well, but they do — it's just delicious! The avocado gives the icing a very creamy texture. Ascorbic or citric acid is added to extend the life of the icing.

Ingredients
2 ripe large Haas avocados
⅛ tsp. (scant) citric or ascorbic acid
½ cup agave nectar
½ cup cocoa powder

1. Peel and pit avocados and scoop pulp into a bowl. Add other ingredients and whisk until all ingredients are incorporated and icing is smooth. Press through a sieve with a rubber spatula to eliminate green flecks.

2. Ice the cooled cake.

Nutritional Information Per Serving
Servings 12 ✳ Calories 105 ✳ Fat 6g ✳ Protein 1g ✳
Carbohydrates 16g ✳ Cholesterol 0mg ✳
Sodium 5mg ✳ Fiber 2g

BAKED ALASKA WITH MERINGUE ICING

BAKED ALASKA

Serve this surprisingly easy dessert when you want to impress your friends, and I promise, they will not suspect this is dairy-free or gluten-free! It is just an elegant, beautiful dessert reserved for special occasions

1. Make one recipe of **"Devilish" Chocolate Cake** (Page 58), but bake it on a 11 x 17 x 1" baking sheet for about 25-30 minutes.

2. Let cool completely and cut into 3" rounds.

3. Place a dome of your favorite dairy-free ice cream on top of the cake rounds (about ½ cup). (Recommend: Rice Dream® Ice Cream.) Place in freezer 30 minutes.

4. Remove from the freezer and pipe **Meringue Icing** (Page 61) "stars" until the cake and ice cream are covered. Place in the freezer 30 minutes.

5. Remove from the freezer and "toast" the meringue with a butane torch, or by placing in the oven at 500°F for about 3 minutes. Serve immediately.

Note: These will keep in the freezer for a couple of days even after the meringues are toasted.

Nutritional Information Per Serving
Servings 15 ✳ Calories 356 ✳ Fat 13g ✳
Protein 3g ✳ Carbohydrates 59g ✳ Cholesterol 0mg ✳
Sodium 455mg ✳ Fiber 2g

MERINGUE ICING

Light, sweet and whipped to perfection. Meringue icing makes anything extra-special. Toasting it with a butane torch or in the broiler gives it that "special touch."

Ingredients

4 egg whites

½ tsp. cream of tartar

½ cup organic cane sugar

½ tsp. Vanilla Powder OR 1 tsp. vanilla

1. Place egg whites in a mixer with the whisk attachment. Beat until foamy. Add cream of tartar and beat until soft peaks form. Add sugar 1 TBS at a time and continue beating until stiff peaks form (about 7-10 minutes on medium speed). Add vanilla powder or vanilla and beat until incorporated.

2. Place meringue in a pastry bag fit with a "star" tip (size 21 or 4B). Pipe stars to decorate. "Toast" with a butane torch or by placing in a 500°F oven for about 3-5 minutes.

Nutritional Information Per Serving

Servings 15 ✻ Calories 30 ✻ Fat 0g ✻ Protein 1g ✻
Carbohydrates 7g ✻ Cholesterol 0mg ✻
Sodium 15mg ✻ Fiber 0g

STRAWBERRY CUPCAKES
WITH CASHEW CREAM ICING

STRAWBERRY CUPCAKES

These delightful pink cupcakes are so good you'll make them over and over.
Freeze-dried strawberries are available in gourmet or natural grocery stores.
They add a beautiful color and rich strawberry taste.

Wet Ingredients

16 raw cashews

½ cup water

½ cup sparkling water

¼ cup agave nectar

¼ cup sunflower oil

2 egg whites

½ cup organic cane sugar

¼ cup ground freeze dried strawberries
 OR 1 TBS beet powder

½ tsp. apple cider vinegar

2 tsp. vanilla

Dry Ingredients

1 cup whole grain sorghum flour

¾ cup whole grain brown rice flour

¼ cup white bean, pinto or navy
bean flour

2 tsp. baking powder

½ tsp. salt

¾ cup whole freeze dried strawberries

PREHEAT OVEN TO 350°F.

1. Put cashews and regular water in a blender and process until smooth. Add remaining wet ingredients and blend until smooth.

2. In a separate bowl, whisk dry ingredients together. Add wet ingredients to dry ingredients. Whisk until incorporated.

3. Pour batter into an oiled muffin pan and fill to the top of each muffin cup. Let batter sit a few minutes to allow flours to absorb the moisture. Bake 25 minutes. Frost with **Cashew Cream Icing** (Page 63). Makes 10-12 cupcakes.

Nutritional Information Per Serving
Servings 12 ✻ Calories 271 ✻ Fat 8g ✻ Protein 4g ✻
Carbohydrates 46g ✻ Cholesterol 0mg ✻
Sodium 180mg ✻ Fiber 3g

CASHEW CREAM ICING

This is an easy, quick-to-make icing.

Ingredients
2 TBS butter substitute
8 raw cashews
¼ cup water
1 tsp. vanilla
3 cups confectioner's sugar

1. In a blender, process cashews, water and butter substitute until smooth. Place in a saucepan. Heat over medium heat until mixture thickens slightly and then add confectioner's sugar and vanilla. Stir until it reaches icing consistency.

2. Ice cooled cupcakes.

Nutritional Information Per Serving
Servings 12 ✳ Calories 149 ✳ Fat 3g ✳ Protein 0g ✳
Carbohydrates 31g ✳ Cholesterol 0mg ✳
Sodium 23mg ✳ Fiber 0g

ORANGE CUPCAKES WITH ORANGE ICING

ORANGE CUPCAKES

Orange oil is the special ingredient for these out-of-the-ordinary cupcakes. The color is delightful, too! It's worth the effort to find the oil, which can be purchased at cake supply or cooking supply stores.

Wet Ingredients

¼ cup orange juice

½ cup rice, nut or seed milk

½ cup sparkling water

¼ cup sunflower oil

2 egg whites*

¾ cup organic cane sugar

1 TBS grated orange zest

1 tsp. orange oil (or a few drops, depending on the taste and oil pungency)

½ cup chopped dried orange slices (optional)

½ cup chopped walnuts

Dry Ingredients

1¼ cups whole grain sorghum flour

¾ cup whole grain brown rice flour

¼ tapioca flour

¼ cup almond meal

½ tsp. allspice

2 tsp. baking powder

½ tsp. salt

PREHEAT OVEN TO 350°F.

1. Combine wet ingredients in a bowl. Mix together until sugar is melted.

2. Separately, whisk dry ingredients together. Add dry ingredients to wet ingredients.

3. Pour batter into an oiled muffin pan and fill to the top of each muffin cup. Let batter sit a few minutes to allow flours to absorb the moisture. Bake 25 minutes.

4. Decorate with a dried orange slice on top, or frost with **Orange Icing** (Page 65). Makes 8-9 cupcakes.

Note: If using dried egg whites, reconstitute with sparkling rather than still water.

Nutritional Information Per Serving
Servings 9 ✳ Calories 331 ✳ Fat 12g ✳ Protein 7g ✳ Carbohydrates 51g ✳ Cholesterol 0mg ✳ Sodium 233mg ✳ Fiber 2g

ORANGE ICING

This is an easy, yet flavorful, adaptation to a simple icing. This unconventional topper will tantalize your taste buds.

1. Make **Cashew Cream Icing** (Page 63).

2. Add: A few drops of orange oil (depending on taste and oil pungency) and 3-4 drops natural orange food coloring.

3. Cool cupcakes, then ice.

Nutritional Information Per Serving
Servings 12 ✳ Calories 149 ✳ Fat 3g ✳ Protein 0g ✳
Carbohydrates 31g ✳ Cholesterol 0mg ✳
Sodium 23mg ✳ Fiber 0g

LEMON BLISS CUPCAKES WITH LEMON GLAZE

LEMON BLISS CUPCAKES

The name says it all — a light, lemony treat to serve to a group of friends with tea, or to make for yourself some afternoon when you need a little zest sprinkled into your day.

Wet Ingredients

¼ cup sunflower oil

2 egg whites

¼ cup agave nectar

½ cup rice, nut or seed milk

½ cup sparkling water

2 tsp. liquid lecithin

½ cup organic cane sugar

1 TBS grated lemon zest

1 tsp. lemon oil (or a few drops, depending on the taste and oil pungency)

½ tsp. apple cider vinegar

2-3 drops natural yellow food coloring (optional)

Dry Ingredients

1 cup whole grain sorghum flour

¾ cup whole grain brown rice flour

⅓ cup whole grain yellow cornmeal

2 tsp. baking powder

½ tsp. salt

PREHEAT OVEN TO 350°F.

1. Combine oil and egg whites in a bowl. Beat with an electric mixer until smooth. Add other wet ingredients and beat 1-2 minutes.

2. Separately, whisk dry ingredients together. Add dry ingredients to wet ingredients.

3. Pour batter into an oiled muffin pan and fill to the top of each muffin cup. Let batter sit a few minutes to allow flours to absorb the moisture. Bake 25 minutes. Glaze cooled muffins with **Lemon Glaze** (Page 67). Makes 9-12 cupcakes.

Nutritional Information Per Serving
Servings 12 ✳ Calories 190 ✳ Fat 6g ✳ Protein 2g ✳ Carbohydrates 33g ✳ Cholesterol 0mg ✳ Sodium 183mg ✳ Fiber 1g

LEMON GLAZE

This not-too-tart simple glaze turns an ordinary cupcake into something special!

Ingredients

2 TBS lemon juice

½ tsp. lemon zest

1 cup confectioner's sugar

1. Whisk ingredients together in a saucepan. Turn heat on high and whisk until smooth and clear. Remove from heat.

2. Poke several holes in the tops of the cupcakes and spoon warm glaze on cooled cupcakes.

Nutritional Information Per Serving

Servings 12 ✳ Calories 150 ✳ Fat 3g ✳ Protein 0g ✳
Carbohydrates 31g ✳ Cholesterol 0mg ✳
Sodium 23mg ✳ Fiber 0g

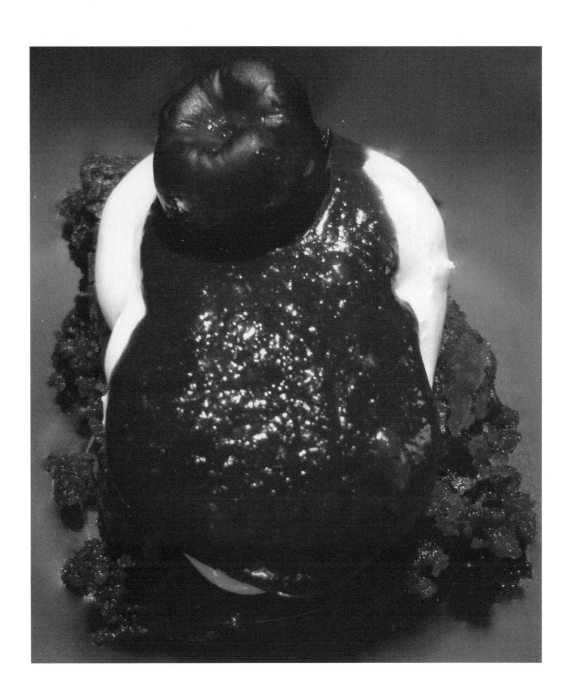

Truffles, Brownies and Bars

From rich, gooey brownies to chewy bars to pop-in-your-mouth truffles and bon bons, these decadent delectables will appear in your dreams.

AMARETTO TRUFFLES WITH CHOCOLATE COATING

AMARETTO TRUFFLES

Truffles are an elegant hand-made holiday present for your special friends. Amaretto, a liqueur made from almonds, adds a romantic flavor. Wrap a handful in brightly colored cellophane or put in an unusual box for a gift just about anyone will enjoy!

Ingredients
½ cup almond butter
½ cup rice syrup
¼ cup cocoa powder
¼ cup amaretto liqueur

Half recipe **"Devilish" Chocolate Layered Cake** (Page 58)

"DEVILISH" CHOCOLATE LAYERED CAKE
(HALF-RECIPE)
Wet Ingredients
2 egg whites
¼ cup butter substitute
½ tsp. liquid lecithin
1 tsp. vanilla
½ cup rice, nut or seed milk
¼ cup plus 2 TBS sparkling water
½ cup organic cane sugar
½ tsp. rice vinegar

Dry Ingredients
¼ cup whole grain sorghum flour
2 TBS whole grain brown rice flour
¼ cup cocoa powder
½ cup arrowroot
¼ cup white rice flour
¼ tsp. xanthan gum
1 tsp. baking soda
½ tsp. baking powder
¼ tsp. salt

1. Make one-half recipe of chocolate cake, following directions on Page 58. (For your convenience, the halved measurements are listed below.)

2. Whisk almond butter, rice syrup, cocoa powder and amaretto in a bowl until smooth. Crumble the cake into the bowl and mix until it is the consistency of stiff cookie dough. Roll into balls and refrigerate 2 hours. Dip into **Chocolate Coating** (Page 71).

Nutritional Information Per Serving
With Chocolate Coating (Page 89):
Servings 40 ✳ Calories 109 ✳ Fat 5g . Protein 1g ✳
Carbohydrates 16g ✳ Cholesterol 0mg ✳
Sodium 75mg ✳ Fiber 1g

CHOCOLATE COATING

This simple recipe works for anything you want to dip in chocolate – for me, that's just about everything! Chocolate chips contain oil, so they melt into a smooth coating that clings well to food. If you use a chocolate bar instead of chips, you'll need to add a little oil, about ⅛ teaspoon per cup.

Ingredients
1 10 oz. package GFCF chocolate chips

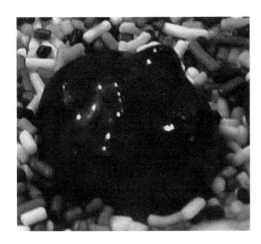

1. Fill the bottom part of a double boiler with water, and place the chips or chocolate in the top half. Be sure the water level doesn't reach the top pan. Melt the chocolate over simmering water, stirring often.

2. Spear the truffle balls with a toothpick and dip into the melted chocolate. Place the end of the toothpick in a Styrofoam™ block until the chocolate hardens.

3. Store in the refrigerator in an airtight container.

BOURBON BON BONS

I served these and mint juleps at a Derby party and they were Blue Ribbon winners with everyone! Distilled alcohol was recently added to the list of "approved" items by several gluten-free societies. Please use at your own discretion.

Ingredients
1 recipe **Angel Food Cake** (Page 54)

⅓ cup hemp seeds
 OR ½ cup raw cashews
½ cup bourbon
2 TBS agave nectar
1 10 oz. package GFCF chocolate chips

1. Cube half of the cooled cake into a bowl. (Freeze the rest for a fast dessert.) Set aside.

2. Blend seeds (or nuts) in a blender with bourbon and agave nectar. Pour over cake mixture. Mix until incorporated. (Add more cake if necessary until the consistency is "formable" but not too "wet".)

3. Form into balls or squares. Chill 2 hours.

4. Melt chocolate chips in a double boiler, stirring until smooth. Dip half of ball or square in chocolate and place on a plate to cool.

Note: These look lovely set in little individual paper cups, as you would find them in a box of fine chocolates.

Nutritional Information Per Serving
Servings 40 ✳ Calories 72 ✳ Fat 3g ✳ Protein 1g ✳
Carbohydrates 11g ✳ Cholesterol 0mg ✳
Sodium 12mg ✳ Fiber 1g

MINI BROWNIES

In our house the corner brownies are the most coveted morsels whenever I bake a batch of these delightful chocolate treats. My husband came up with the idea to bake the brownies in a mini-muffin pan. It controls portion size and everyone gets that crispy-on-the-outside and chewy-on-the-inside goodness.

Wet Ingredients

½ cup sunflower oil

¾ cup sugar

3 egg whites

1 tsp. vanilla

½ tsp. cider vinegar

Dry Ingredients

⅓ cup cocoa powder

¼ cup whole grain sorghum flour

2 TBS cornstarch, sweet rice or tapioca flour

2 TBS soy or gafava flour

½ tsp. xanthan gum

¼ tsp. plus ⅛ tsp. baking powder

1 tsp. coffee crystals

PREHEAT OVEN TO 350°F.

1. Beat together the wet ingredients.

2. Whisk dry ingredients together and mix with wet ingredients.

3. Divide into an oiled mini-muffin pan and bake 18 minutes. Makes 15 mini brownies. (If you use a regular muffin pan bake 25 minutes; makes 12 brownies.)

Nutritional Information Per Serving
Servings 15 ✳ Calories 129 ✳ Fat 8g ✳ Protein 2g ✳
Carbohydrates 15g ✳ Cholesterol 0mg ✳
Sodium 27mg ✳ Fiber 1g

BLACK FOREST BROWNIES (VEGAN)

Chocolate, dark cherries and walnuts – a luscious combination of flavors! Mmmmm! These rich brownies are egg-less.

Flax Mix
⅔ cup water
2 TBS flax seeds

Wet Ingredients
¼ cup non-dairy mayonnaise
1 cup organic cane sugar
2 tsp. vanilla
½ tsp. guar gum

Dry Ingredients
⅓ cup cocoa powder
¼ cup whole grain sorghum flour
¼ cup whole grain brown rice flour
¼ cup plus 2 TBS arrowroot
½ cup GFCF chocolate chips
½ cup dried Bing cherries
¼ cup chopped walnuts
1 tsp. baking powder
1 tsp. xanthan gum
⅛ tsp. salt

PREHEAT OVEN TO 350°F.

1. Process flax seeds and water in a blender until smooth. In a separate bowl, beat wet ingredients together, then add Flax Mix.

2. In a separate bowl, whisk dry ingredients together. Mix dry ingredients with wet ingredients.

3. Place in an 8 x 8 x 2" oiled pan and bake 25-30 minutes.

Nutritional Information Per Serving
Servings 25 ✳ Calories 127 ✳ Fat 6g ✳ Protein 1g ✳
Carbohydrates 19g ✳ Cholesterol 0mg ✳
Sodium 56mg ✳ Fiber 1g

BLONDIES

Even die-hard chocoholics may get hooked on these tasty bites! (If you really miss the chocolate, you could add ½ cup of chocolate chips to this recipe.)

Wet Ingredients

3 egg whites
½ cup butter substitute or walnut oil
¾ cup organic cane sugar
1 tsp. vanilla

Dry Ingredients

⅓ cup whole grain sorghum flour
¼ cup whole grain brown rice flour
2 TBS tapioca flour
½ tsp. baking powder
½ tsp. xanthan gum (omit if using **"Margarine"** (Page 213) as the butter substitute)
½ cup chopped pecans (optional)

PREHEAT OVEN TO 350°F.

1. Beat wet ingredients together.

2. In a separate bowl, whisk dry ingredients together.

3. Combine dry ingredients with wet ingredients.

4. Bake in an oiled 8 x 8 x 2" baking pan 30-35 minutes, covering the top with parchment after 20 minutes to prevent over-browning.

Nutritional Information Per Serving
Servings 25 ✳ Calories 88 ✳ Fat 5g ✳ Protein 1g ✳
Carbohydrates 10g ✳ Cholesterol 0mg ✳
Sodium 59mg ✳ Fiber 0g

SKUNKS

This three-layered delight is a version of a family favorite when I was growing up. My dad used to eat the last one and leave a note "the phantom strikes again." (That phantom sure liked chocolate!) Spooning the dark icing down the length of the cream makes it look like the back of a skunk. These would be fun to serve at a kid's party.

Ingredients
1 recipe **Black Forest Brownies** (Page 74)
1 13 oz. jar marshmallow cream
1 batch **Tahini Icing** (Page 47)

Confectioner's sugar

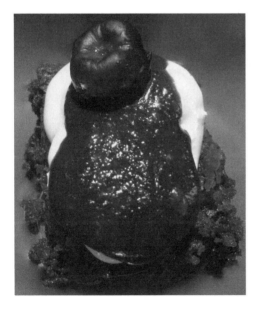

1. Use two cooled brownies per "skunk."

2. Place brownies on a plate, and spread with marshmallow cream. Sprinkle each brownie with a little confectioner's sugar to make it easier to spread the marshmallow cream.

3. Spoon a stripe of Tahini Icing down the middle of the marshmallow cream. Top with a cherry.

Nutritional Information Per Serving
Servings 12 ✳ Calories 517 ✳ Fat 24 ✳ Protein 6g ✳
Carbohydrates 72g ✳ Cholesterol 0mg ✳
Sodium 153mg ✳ Fiber 4g

PEANUT BUTTER / CHOCOLATE CHIP BARS

Peanut butter and chocolate…a sensational combination! These hearty, rich bars are a nice treat tucked into a lunch bag or taken to an outdoor sporting event.

Wet Ingredients

½ cup sunflower oil

⅔ cup crunchy peanut butter

4 egg whites

Dry Ingredients

⅔ cup whole grain sorghum flour

⅓ cup whole grain brown rice flour

⅓ cup tapioca flour, cornstarch or arrowroot

½ cup Sucanat®

½ cup organic cane sugar

2 tsp. baking powder

½ tsp. salt

1 tsp. xanthan gum

⅔ cup GFCF chocolate chips

PREHEAT OVEN TO 350°F.

1. Mix wet ingredients. In a separate bowl, whisk dry ingredients together. Combine dry with wet and mix until incorporated. Fold in chocolate chips.

2. Press dough into an oiled, nonstick 8 x 8" baking pan. Bake 25-30 minutes.

Nutritional Information Per Serving

Servings 25 ✳ Calories 166 ✳ Fat 10g ✳
Protein 3g ✳ Carbohydrates 19g ✳ Cholesterol 0mg ✳
Sodium 126mg ✳ Fiber 1g

PEANUT BUTTER / CHOCOLATE CHIP BARS (VEGAN)

This egg-less, vegan version makes a scrumptious bar. Same great taste with only a slight difference in texture. A comparison of the two versions follows.

Wet Ingredients

½ cup warm water

8 tsp. soy protein isolate

½ tsp. agar powder

½ cup sunflower oil

⅔ cup crunchy peanut butter

Dry Ingredients

⅔ cup whole grain sorghum flour

⅓ cup whole grain brown rice flour

⅓ cup tapioca flour, cornstarch or arrowroot

½ cup Sucanat®

½ cup organic cane sugar

2 tsp. baking powder

1 tsp. xanthan gum

½ tsp. sea salt

⅔ cup GFCF chocolate chips

PREHEAT OVEN TO 350°F.

1. Place water, soy protein isolate and agar powder in a bowl and whip until foamy. Add other wet ingredients.

2. In a separate bowl, whisk dry ingredients together. Combine dry with wet and mix until incorporated. Fold in chocolate chips.

3. Press dough into an oiled, nonstick 8 x 8" baking pan. Bake 25-30 minutes.

Nutritional Information Per Serving
Servings 25 ✳ Calories 165 ✳ Fat 10 ✳ Protein 2g ✳
Carbohydrates 19g ✳ Cholesterol 0mg ✳
Sodium 119mg ✳ Fiber 1g

COMPARISON:
PEANUT BUTTER / CHOCOLATE CHIP BARS

EGG WHITES
versus
SOY PROTEIN ISOLATE

The recipe was followed exactly the same except in one, egg whites were used, and in the other, soy protein isolate and agar powder was used. Bars were baked in the same oven, using the same size pan at the same temperature.

With Egg Whites

* Great taste

* Nice cake-like texture, yet still with the chewy bar mouth feel

* Rose more than soy protein isolate bars

* Respectable, would serve to company

With Soy Protein Isolate

* Great taste

* Passable texture and crumb consistency; a little crisper, a little denser

* Rose less than bars made with egg whites

* Respectable, would serve to company

Both batches were good and got great reviews from tasters. (Proving once again, chocolate and peanut butter are a winning combination!)

SAVORY SEEDY SENSATIONS WITH PUMPKIN SEED BUTTER

SAVORY SEED SENSATIONS

Having a savory bar in your arsenal of baked goodies is a refreshing change. These make a great mid-afternoon snack and are a hearty compliment to a soup or salad.

Wet Ingredients

½ cup sunflower oil

⅔ cup Pumpkin Seed Butter

2 TBS toasted sunflower seeds (reserve 1 tsp.)

2 TBS toasted sesame seeds (reserve 1 tsp.)

2 TBS hemp seeds (reserve 1 tsp.)

4 egg whites

Dry Ingredients

⅔ cup whole grain sorghum flour

⅓ cup whole grain brown rice flour

⅓ cup tapioca flour, cornstarch or arrowroot

1 tsp. xanthan gum

2 tsp. baking powder

½ tsp. garlic salt

2 TBS vegetable bouillon powder (preferably with no salt, onion, oil or sugar added)

PREHEAT OVEN TO 350°F.

1. Mix wet ingredients in a bowl.

2. In a separate bowl, whisk dry ingredients together. Combine the dry with wet and mix until incorporated.

3. Press into an oiled 8 x 8" pan. Top with reserved seeds. Bake 25-30 minutes.

Nutritional Information Per Serving
Servings 16 ✳ Calories 190 ✳ Fat 14g ✳ Protein 5g ✳ Carbohydrates 13g ✳ Cholesterol 0mg ✳ Sodium 190mg ✳ Fiber 1g

PUMPKIN SEED BUTTER

This simple, easy pumpkin butter is an oh-so-satisfying spread on a cracker. Once you taste the homemade version you'll never use store-bought again! Pumpkin seeds contain essential amino acids, and are a good source of zinc, iron, protein and fiber. Store raw pumpkin seeds in the refrigerator or freezer.

Ingredients

1 cup raw pumpkin seeds
2 TBS sunflower oil
¼ tsp. salt

1. Toast pumpkin seeds according to the directions on (Page 212). Remove from heat and cool.

2. Place seeds, oil and salt into a food processor and process until smooth. Yields approximately ⅔ cup.

3. Store pumpkin butter in an airtight container in the refrigerator. Best if used within 7 days.

Nutritional Information Per Serving
Servings 16 ✳ Calories 33 ✳ Fat 2g ✳ Protein 1g ✳
Carbohydrates 2g ✳ Cholesterol 0mg ✳
Sodium 34mg ✳ Fiber 1g

RAISIN BARS

Try these sweet and spicy raisin bars dusted with confectioner's sugar at your next gathering. Allspice lends flavors of cinnamon, cloves and nutmeg, but it's not a spice blend. It is the dried fruit of a plant, found in the West Indies, Central America and southern Mexico.

Wet Ingredients

¼ cup walnut or sunflower oil
2 egg whites
¾ cup Sucanat® or brown sugar
½ tsp. apple cider vinegar

Raisins

½ cup apple juice concentrate
¼ cup water
1 cup raisins
1 tsp. allspice
1 tsp. cinnamon

Dry Ingredients

¾ cup whole grain teff flour
¾ cup whole grain sorghum flour
½ cup whole grain brown rice flour
½ tsp. xanthan gum
2 tsp. baking powder
½ tsp. salt

Confectioner's sugar for dusting

PREHEAT OVEN TO 350°F.

1. In a stand mixer, combine wet ingredients.

2. In a covered pot, simmer raisins, water and spices in apple juice concentrate until raisins are plump (about 2 minutes). Cool.

3. Whisk dry ingredients together in a bowl. Add to wet ingredients. Add raisins and apple juice concentrate.

4. Place in an oiled, non-stick 8 x 8" pan. Bake 30-35 minutes. Remove from the oven and dust the top with confectioner's sugar.

Nutritional Information Per Serving
Servings 20 ✳ Calories 134 ✳ Fat 4g ✳ Protein 2g ✳
Carbohydrates 24g ✳ Cholesterol 0mg ✳
Sodium 113mg ✳ Fiber 2g

DATE STREUSEL BARS

I once purchased something like these in a Canadian grocery store and have tried to perfect the recipe ever since. Finally — here it is. These bars are fast to make and satisfy everyone's craving for an evening morsel. Dates are super-healthy, containing a variety of B-vitamins and more potassium than bananas!

Ingredients

Streusel

1 cup whole grain sorghum flour

1 cup flaked grain (GF oats, rice, quinoa, millet or buckwheat flakes)

½ cup Sucanat®, date sugar or brown sugar

½ cup sunflower oil

Tiny pinch of salt

Date Filling

1 cup pitted dates (halved and pressed into a measuring cup to measure)

¼ cup maple syrup

¼ cup chopped slivered almonds or chopped walnuts (optional)

PREHEAT OVEN TO 350°F.

1. Mix streusel together in a bowl.

2. Press half of the streusel in an 8 x 8" oiled baking pan.

3. In a food processor, process the dates and maple syrup until smooth. Add nuts. Press on top of the streusel.

4. Place the other half of the streusel on top of the dates and press down. Bake 25-35 minutes or until lightly browned. Cool, cut and serve.

Nutritional Information Per Serving
Servings 20 ✳ Calories 145 ✳ Fat 7g ✳ Protein 2g ✳
Carbohydrates 21g ✳ Cholesterol 0mg ✳
Sodium 14mg ✳ Fiber 1g

Desserts

In our home, a meal just isn't complete without dessert. Whether it's a light, airy soufflé, a velvety rich pudding, or a fresh berry soufflé, a little something sweet ends dinner on a high note and makes you leave the table satisfied. Bake one of these delights tonight!

Strawberry Soufflés, 86

Mocha Soufflés, 87

Chocolate Attack with Chocolate Pudding and Whipped Cream (Vegan), 88

Elegant Bread Pudding with Sweet Cashew Cream Sauce, 90

Elegant Bread Pudding with Sweet Cashew Cream Sauce (Vegan), 92

✳ Comparison: Elegant Bread Pudding
Egg Whites versus Hemp Seed Cream, 93

Apple Cherry Bread Pudding, 94

Chocolate Roll, 95

Fruit Custard, 96

Baked Custard, 97

Lady Fingers, 98

STRAWBERRY SOUFFLÉS

Fresh strawberry soufflés are a fat-free, low calorie delightful summer treat. Make ahead and bake them while you are eating dinner. The "one serving" version is a perfect dessert when you are cooking for yourself and want an elegant treat. Serve directly from the oven.

Ingredients

One Serving	Six Servings
3	12 fresh or frozen strawberries (thawed)
2 tsp.	3 TBS agave nectar
1	6 egg whites
2 TBS	½ cup organic cane sugar
1⁄16 tsp.	¼ tsp. vanilla powder*

PREHEAT OVEN TO 375°F.

1. Process strawberries and agave nectar in food processor until pureed.

2. Meanwhile, in a stand mixer with the whisk attachment, beat egg whites until soft peaks form. Add sugar a little at a time, and continue beating on medium speed until stiff and silky. Add vanilla powder. Manually fold in strawberry puree.

3. Pour into small, individual oiled and sugared ramekins (3¼" diameter x 2" high). Smooth the top and run your finger around the edges to clean. Bake in the middle of the oven 15 minutes, until golden brown. Serve immediately.

*Vanilla powder is used in this recipe as a stabilizer as well as adding a wonderful vanilla taste.

Nutritional Information Per Serving
Servings 1 ✳ Calories 163 ✳ Fat 0g ✳ Protein 4g ✳ Carbohydrates 38g ✳ Cholesterol 0mg ✳ Sodium 72mg ✳ Fiber 1g

ALTERNATIVE COOK, LLC™

MOCHA SOUFFLÉS

A little sweet, a little bitter, and rich with chocolate flavor — just the right combination in a light dessert. What could be a better ending to a fabulous meal? Let this become a regular (high-protein) all occasion dessert in your home.

Ingedients

One Serving	Six Servings
1 tsp.	3 TBS cocoa powder
¼ tsp.	2 tsp. instant coffee crystals
1 TBS	⅓ cup agave nectar
1	6 egg whites
1 TBS	⅓ cup organic cane sugar
¹⁄₁₆ tsp.	¼ tsp. vanilla powder

PREHEAT OVEN TO 375°F.

1. In a bowl, make a chocolate sauce by combining the agave nectar, coffee crystals and cocoa powder. Whisk until dissolved. Set aside.

2. Meanwhile, in a stand mixer with the whisk attachment, beat egg whites until soft peaks form. Add sugar, a little at a time and continue beating on medium speed until egg whites are stiff and silky. Add vanilla powder. Manually fold in chocolate sauce.

3. Pour into small, individual oiled and sugared ramekins (3¼" diameter x 2" high). Smooth the top, and run your finger around the edges to clean. Bake in the middle of the oven 15 minutes, until golden brown. Serve immediately.

*Vanilla powder is used in this recipe as a stabilizer as well as adding a wonderful vanilla taste.

Nutritional Information Per Serving
Servings 1 ✳ Calories 156 ✳ Fat 0g ✳ Protein 4g ✳
Carbohydrates 37g ✳ Cholesterol 0mg ✳
Sodium 72mg ✳ Fiber 1g

CHOCOLATE ATTACK WITH CHOCOLATE PUDDING AND WHIPPED CREAM

CHOCOLATE ATTACK

This may be one of the most decadent, delicious desserts you'll ever make! The delightful combination of chocolate, strawberries and marshmallow topped with an innovative Whipped Cream to serve at your next dinner party, and I promise you'll be very popular!

Ingredients

1 recipe **"Devilish" Chocolate Layered Cake** (Page 58), baked in 3 layers

1 recipe **Chocolate Pudding** (Page 89)

1 cup fresh strawberries, chopped
1 13 oz. jar marshmallow cream
1 9.7 oz. GFCF dark chocolate

Whipped Cream (Page 89)

1. Place one layer of the cake in a large glass bowl. On top of cake, place one-third of the pudding, strawberries, marshmallow cream and chopped chocolate, in that order. Continue to layer starting first with the cake until all ingredients are used.

2. Chill 2 hours and serve, topped with Whipped Cream.

Nutritional Information Per Serving
Servings 12 ✳ Calories 487 ✳ Fat 17g ✳
Protein 5g ✳ Carbohydrates 80g ✳ Cholesterol 0mg ✳
Sodium 483mg ✳ Fiber 5g

ALTERNATIVE COOK, LLC™

CHOCOLATE PUDDING

This smooth, creamy and yes, fat-free pudding hits the spot when you need a chocolate fix and not a lot of calories! Go ahead – indulge!

Ingredients

2 cups rice, nut or seed milk
¼ cup cocoa powder
½ cup whole grain sorghum flour
¼ cup organic cane sugar
 OR ⅛ tsp. stevia
2 tsp. vanilla
⅛ tsp. coffee crystals
Tiny pinch of salt

1. Whisk ingredients together in a saucepan, heat on high, stirring constantly until mixture thickens.

2. Place in individual serving dishes, serve warm or cover with plastic wrap and chill 2 hours.

Nutritional Information Per Serving
Servings 4 ✳ Calories 154 ✳ Fat 2g ✳ Protein 2g ✳ Carbohydrates 34g ✳ Cholesterol 0mg ✳ Sodium 45mg ✳ Fiber 2g

WHIPPED CREAM (VEGAN)

Soy protein isolate whips like egg whites if you add a little stabilizer. This vegan whipped topping can be spooned or piped - just as you would with traditional whipped cream.

Ingredients

½ cup warm water
1 tsp. agar powder
¼ cup soy protein isolate
1 tsp. vanilla powder*
¼ cup organic cane sugar

Vanilla powder is used in this recipe as a stabilizer as well as adding a wonderful vanilla taste.

1. Using a stand mixer with the whisk attachment, dissolve agar in water on low speed. Add soy protein and vanilla powder. Increase speed and slowly add sugar. Beat until peaks stay standing when mixer is turned off, about 10-12 minutes.

2. Place mixture in a piping bag and decorate desserts when ready to serve. (This does not last in the refrigerator.) Makes about 3 cups.

Nutritional Information Per Serving
Servings 24 ✳ Calories 21 ✳ Fat 0g ✳ Protein 0g ✳ Carbohydrates 0g ✳ Cholesterol 0mg ✳ Sodium 0mg ✳ Fiber 0g

ELEGANT BREAD PUDDING WITH SWEET CASHEW CREAM SAUCE

ELEGANT BREAD PUDDING

You wouldn't normally associate the word "elegant" with bread pudding, but you may change your mind after making this version with the sweet cream sauce. It turns a rather mundane dessert into something special. A variety of breads make the best pudding! A vegan version of the recipe follows, and both are compared for taste and texture.

Ingredients
Bread
8 slices gluten-free bread*

Egg Mixture
12 egg whites
1 cup rice, nut or seed milk
2 tsp. vanilla
1 cup organic cane sugar or xylitol**
2 tsp. cinnamon
¼ tsp. freshly ground nutmeg

*Montina® Sandwich Bread (Page 143) is good in this recipe, or combine a variety of different kinds of bread.

**Xylitol takes some getting used to. Substitute one teaspoon at a time for the cane sugar until your body gets used to it.

PREHEAT OVEN TO 350°F.

1. Cube bread, including crust, and place in an oiled 8 x 8" baking dish.

2. Separately, beat egg whites until foamy. Add the rest of the ingredients in the Egg Mixture and mix together. Pour egg mixture over bread cubes.

3. Prepare a water bath: Place an empty baking pan on oven rack, add baking dish with bread pudding, then slowly pour hot water into pan until it is ½" deep. Bake 45-50 minutes. Serve warm or cooled with **Sweet Cashew Cream Sauce** (Page 91).

Nutritional Information Per Serving
Servings 8 ✳ Calories 204 ✳ Fat 1g ✳ Protein 7g ✳
Carbohydrates 41g ✳ Cholesterol 0mg ✳
Sodium 228mg ✳ Fiber 1g

SWEET CASHEW CREAM SAUCE

This nut-chunky cream sauce pares well with the texture of the bread pudding. Serve it on the side in a pretty bowl, or spoon a little on top of each serving of the pudding.

Ingredients
Cream
½ cup raw cashews OR hemp seeds OR any raw nut or seed
1 cup water
¼ cup Sucanat® or xylitol
2 tsp. vanilla
½ tsp. umeboshi vinegar

¼ cup **Ume Plum Cashews** (Page 171)

1. Combine Cream ingredients in a blender and process 2-3 minutes until smooth. Place in a saucepan and cook over high heat until the consistency of thick cream, whisking constantly.

2. Add **Ume Plum Cashews** or ¼ cup pre-purchased salted whole cashews. Serve sauce warm over warm bread pudding.

*Note: If allergic to nuts, make the sauce using hemp seeds and omit the **Ume Plum Cashews.***

Extra sauce can be refrigerated up to 7 days.

Nutritional Information Per Serving
Servings 8 ✳ Calories 221 ✳ Fat 9g ✳ Protein 3g ✳
Carbohydrates 35g ✳ Cholesterol 0mg ✳
Sodium 4mg ✳ Fiber 1g

ELEGANT BREAD PUDDING (VEGAN)

Here's one dessert where you might like the vegan version even better than its egg-white laden counterpart! The nut or seed cream substitution adds a rich, satisfying background flavor to the pudding. Both versions are compared on (Page 93).

Ingredients
Bread
8 slices gluten-free bread*

Seed or Nut Mixture
1⅓ cups water
½ cup hemp seeds OR any raw nut or seed
1 cup rice, nut or seed milk
2 tsp. vanilla
1 cup organic cane sugar or xylitol**
2 tsp. cinnamon
¼ tsp. freshly ground nutmeg

*****Montina® Sandwich Bread** (Page 143) is good in this recipe, or combine a variety of different kinds of bread.*

*****Xylitol takes some getting used to. Substitute one teaspoon at a time for the cane sugar until your body gets used to it.*

PREHEAT OVEN TO 350°F.

1. Cube bread, including crust, and place in an oiled 8 x 8" baking dish.

2. Place Seed or Nut Mixture ingredients in a blender and process until smooth. Pour mixture over bread cubes.

3. Prepare a water bath: Place an empty baking pan on oven rack, add baking dish with bread pudding, then slowly pour hot water into pan until it is ½" deep. Bake 45-50 minutes. Serve warm or cooled with **Sweet Cashew Cream Sauce** (Page 91).

Nutritional Information Per Serving
Servings 8 ✳ Calories 231 ✳ Fat 6g ✳ Protein 4g ✳ Carbohydrates 42g ✳ Cholesterol 0mg ✳ Sodium 146mg ✳ Fiber 2g

COMPARISON:
ELEGANT BREAD PUDDING

EGG WHITES
versus
HEMP SEED CREAM

The recipe was followed the same except one was made with egg whites and the other was made with a hemp seed cream. Both were made with xylitol, as was the Cashew Cream. This recipe is also known as my Xylitol Lesson. I'd been eating 1-2 TBS of xylitol with no problem, but the vegan pudding tasted so good, I ate the whole serving (which had about ¼ cup of xylitol), and a few hours later, I was really sorry! So, please incorporate it into your diet slowly.

With Egg Whites

✳ Nice taste, on the lighter side.

✳ Crunchy on top and creamy pudding texture inside.

✳ Would present this pudding to company.

With Hemp Seed Cream

✳ Rich taste. Pleasant taste of the hemp seeds comes through.

✳ Crunchy on top and creamy pudding texture inside.

✳ Would present this pudding to company. (Both are good, but I preferred this one.)

Cashew Cream Sauce – Delightful!

APPLE CHERRY BREAD PUDDING

A fruity bread pudding is a pleasing dessert but it's also a great breakfast food! Use up those last few pieces of day-old bread or make a loaf just for pudding. Add some apples and cherries (or your own combination of fruit) and serve warm. This recipe features stevia, a natural plant sweetener. Stevia is extremely sweet and a tiny bit goes a long way!

Ingredients

Cashew Cream

2 cups water

¾ cups raw cashews

Apple Mixture

2 peeled, chopped apples

24 dried Bing cherries

½ cup frozen apple juice concentrate, thawed

¼ tsp. stevia

2 TBS butter substitute

1 tsp. cinnamon

½ tsp. freshly ground nutmeg

2 tsp. vanilla

4 egg whites

Dry Ingredients

6-7 cups (day-old) GF bread*

PREHEAT OVEN TO 350°F.

1. Cube bread into a large mixing bowl.

2. To make Cream: place cashews and water into a blender and process until smooth.

3. In a saucepan, combine the apples, cherries, stevia and butter substitute with the thawed apple juice concentrate. Add cinnamon and nutmeg. Simmer slowly until apples and cherries are plump. Remove from heat and add vanilla.

4. In a separate bowl, whisk egg whites until foamy. Add cashew milk and the apple mixture. Pour over dry ingredients and mix.

5. Place pudding into an oiled 8 x 8" glass baking pan. Bake 40-45 minutes. Delicious warm or cold. Top the warm pudding with a scoop of your favorite dairy-free ice cream for a scrumptious dessert!

** I like to use Breads From Anna's yeast-free, gluten-free loaf OR one recipe **Vegan No-yeast Whole Grain Buns** (Page 144) in this recipe, but any assortment of bread can be used.*

Nutritional Information Per Serving
Servings 12 ✳ Calories 351 ✳ Fat 11g ✳
Protein 9g ✳ Carbohydrates 58g ✳ Cholesterol 0mg ✳
Sodium 225mg ✳ Fiber 7g

CHOCOLATE ROLL

Chocolate cake rolled around rich, shaved, high-quality chocolate and dusted with cocoa powder – this is heaven! The recipe calls for Scharffen Berger's chocolate, available at gourmet groceries and cooking stores but any high-quality chocolate can be used. Now, this is my idea of dessert!

Wet Ingredients

4 eggs, separated
½ tsp. cream of tartar
¾ cup organic cane sugar
2 tsp. vanilla

Dry Ingredients

3 TBS whole grain sorghum flour
3 TBS sweet rice flour
3 TBS cornstarch
3 TBS cocoa powder
1½ tsp. xanthan gum
1 tsp. baking powder
¼ tsp. salt

½ cup shaved Scharffen Berger's 70% semi-sweet chocolate (reserve 1 TBS)
Cocoa powder for dusting

PREHEAT OVEN TO 400°F.

1. Prepare a 11 x 17 x 1" cookie sheet by lining with parchment, spraying with spray-on oil and lightly dusting with cocoa powder.

2. Separate egg whites and yolks. With the whisk attachment, beat the egg whites until foamy. Add cream of tartar and beat until stiff, gradually adding half of the sugar, one TBS at a time, and then the vanilla. Set aside.

3. In a separate bowl, whisk dry together ingredients.

4. Place egg yolks in a mixer with a paddle beater. Beat the yolks until thick and bright yellow, adding the remaining sugar. Fold yolk mixture into egg whites. Then fold in dry ingredients.

5. Spread batter on prepared pan until about ¾" thick. Bake 10-15 minutes until golden brown. Remove from oven and turn over on a new piece of parchment paper sprayed with oil and sprinkled with cocoa powder. Carefully remove baking parchment. Cover with shaved chocolate. Starting at shorter side, roll cake. Let cool while rolled up. Slice and serve.

Nutritional Information Per Serving
Servings 10 ✳ Calories 173 ✳ Fat 6g ✳ Protein 4g ✳
Carbohydrates 30g ✳ Cholesterol 85mg ✳
Sodium 79mg ✳ Fiber 2g

FRUIT CUSTARD

Warm, creamy custard with peaches and granola — this is definitely comfort food in our house. Serve it as an after-dinner dessert or halve the sugar and serve it for breakfast. Everyone will love its warm, soul-satisfying goodness!

Ingredients

2 cups rice, nut or seed milk

4 egg whites

½ cup whole grain brown rice flour

2 tsp. vanilla

½ cup organic cane sugar

¼ tsp. freshly ground nutmeg

½ tsp. cinnamon

2 cups chopped peaches*

1 cup Granola (Page 184)

PREHEAT OVEN TO 350°F.

1. Mix together all ingredients except granola in a bowl.

2. Pour into a medium-sized oiled baking dish or four individual ramekins. Sprinkle with granola.

3. Bake 45-50 minutes or until warm and bubbly.

* Peaches can be fresh (peel before chopping), or from a jar or can (drain before using).

Nutritional Information Per Serving
Servings 4 ✳ Calories 428 ✳ Fat 10g ✳
Protein 11g ✳ Carbohydrates 76g ✳ Cholesterol 0mg ✳
Sodium 127mg ✳ Fiber 5g

BAKED CUSTARD

Baked custards are best served directly from the oven. Their heart-warming taste and creamy texture is oh-so satisfying!

Ingredients
Cashew Cream
2 cups water
¾ cup raw cashews

Custard
5 egg whites
⅓ cup organic cane sugar or Florida Crystals®
1 tsp. vanilla
1 TBS Courvoisier or brandy (optional)
Freshly ground nutmeg

PREHEAT OVEN TO 350°F.

1. Make the Cashew Cream: place water and cashews in a blender and process until smooth. Strain into a saucepan and cook over high heat, stirring constantly/frequently until it turns into a thick cream (and coats the back of a spoon).

2. Make the Custard: whisk egg whites until foamy in a mixer and slowly add sugar 1 TBS at a time. When soft peaks form, fold in vanilla and brandy (optional).

3. Add cashew cream to the custard mixer. Whisk 10 seconds then divide custard into four individual ramekins. Top each with a sprinkling of freshly ground nutmeg.

4. Place ramekins in a baking pan and fill pan with 1" of water. Bake 45-50 minutes. Custard is done when an inserted knife comes out clean.

Nutritional Information Per Serving
Servings 4 ✻ Calories 173 ✻ Fat 12g ✻ Protein 8g ✻
Carbohydrates 8g ✻ Cholesterol 0 mg ✻
Sodium 76mg ✻ Fiber 1g

LADY FINGERS

Lady Fingers are low calorie, low fat, elegant cookies that don't get featured nearly as much as they should. These crisp treats marry just beautifully with fruit, or as a special crust in a Lady Finger cake. Powdered egg whites work equally well in this recipe.

Egg Whites

3 egg whites or reconstituted powdered egg white equivalent

¼ tsp. cream of tartar

⅓ cup organic cane sugar

1 tsp. vanilla

Wet Ingredients

1 tsp. sunflower or walnut oil

½ tsp. liquid lecithin

Dry Ingredients

⅓ cup whole grain sorghum flour

¼ cup whole grain brown rice flour

2 TBS cornstarch

¾ tsp. xanthan gum

Tiny pinch of salt

Confectioner's sugar

PREHEAT OVEN TO 350°F.

1. Beat egg whites until foamy. Add cream of tartar. Continue beating, adding sugar one TBS at a time, until stiff peaks form. Add vanilla. Set aside.

2. In a separate bowl, using a hand mixer, emulsify wet ingredients.

3. Add dry ingredients to wet and mix until incorporated. (This will be very dry.) Fold mixture into egg whites being careful not to over mix.

4. Place batter into a piping bag fitted with the large star tip (1M). Pipe 3-4" long fingers on a Silpat. Bake 12-15 minutes. Sprinkle with confectioner's sugar and remove from Silpat while still warm. Place on a rack to cool.

Nutritional Information Per Serving
Servings 24 ✳ Calories 36 ✳ Fat 0g ✳ Protein 1g ✳
Carbohydrates 7g ✳ Cholesterol 0mg ✳
Sodium 7mg ✳ Fiber 0g

Cookies

From all-American oatmeal cookies to gingerbread or chocolate chip – cookies are one of the best foods when you need a little something to perk you up. And what could be more welcoming than a homemade warm cookie? These recipes are sure to be "standards" in your household.

OATMEAL CHOCOLATE RAISIN COOKIES (VEGAN)

Not all oats are gluten-free! Please be sure your package says "gluten-free", and incorporate them into your diet slowly (with doctor supervision). Try adding some GF cereal in addition to, or instead of, the oats for a nice variation. I love these cookies for breakfast or an afternoon snack. You could use regular raisins, but the chocolate-covered raisins make these extra-special.

Wet Ingredients

½ cup rice syrup

4 oz. unsweetened applesauce

3 teaspoons Ener-G® egg substitute and 4 TBS water OR 3 egg whites

1 cup date sugar OR Sucanat® or brown sugar

¼ cup organic cane sugar OR ¼ tsp. stevia

1 tsp. vanilla

2 TBS sunflower oil

4 TBS water

Dry Ingredients

1 cup whole grain sorghum flour

½ cup whole grain brown rice flour

1½ tsp. cinnamon

½ tsp. salt

1 tsp. baking soda

3 cups GF oats

 OR: 1½ cups GF oats and 1½ cups crushed GF cereal

 OR: 3 cups crushed GF cereal

1½ cups GFCF chocolate covered raisins

PREHEAT OVEN TO 350°F.

1. Combine wet and dry ingredients (except chocolate raisins) in a stand mixer. Mix until incorporated.

2. Fold in the chocolate covered raisins. Form into 2" balls and flatten slightly on a Silpat.

3. Bake 13-15 minutes.

Nutritional Information Per Serving

Servings 32 ✳ Calories 178 ✳ Fat 4g ✳ Protein 4g ✳ Carbohydrates 32g ✳ Cholesterol 0mg ✳ Sodium 118mg ✳ Fiber 3g

PEANUT BUTTER COOKIES

Growing up, these cookies were one of my favorites. Not much has changed! These chewy cookies smell fantastic while baking and make a perfect after school or work snack (if they last that long!). If you are avoiding peanuts, try almond butter or **Pumpkin Seed Butter** *(Page 81) for an equally flavorsome morsel.*

Wet Ingredients

½ cup crunchy peanut butter

1 cup maple sugar (not syrup)
 OR organic cane sugar or Sucanat®

2 tsp. vanilla

3 egg whites

¼ cup sunflower oil

1 tsp. liquid lecithin

⅓ cup vanilla rice, nut or seed milk

Dry Ingredients

1½ cups whole grain sorghum flour

1¼ cup whole grain brown rice flour

⅓ cup tapioca flour

1½ tsp. xanthan gum

2 tsp. baking powder

½ tsp. salt

2 TBS organic cane sugar (for dipping dough before baking)

PREHEAT OVEN TO 350°F.

1. In a stand mixer, combine wet ingredients.

2. In a separate bowl, whisk dry ingredients together and add to wet ingredients. Mix until incorporated.

3. Oil hands and form into 2" sized balls and dip into sugar. Place on a Silpat or oiled baking sheet. Flatten out and press the tops crisscross with a fork. Bake 15 minutes.

Nutritional Information Per Serving
Servings 24 ✳ Calories 162 ✳ Fat 6g ✳ Protein 3g ✳ Carbohydrates 25g ✳ Cholesterol 0mg ✳ Sodium 121mg ✳ Fiber 1g

SUGAR COOKIES

Here's your staple sugar cookie that you'll bake again and again. The dough works well in a cookie press or can be rolled out, cut into shapes and decorated for various holidays. Keep dough in the freezer for a fast batch anytime. Make 'em little, make 'em big – just make them!

Wet Ingredients

½ cup walnut, sunflower oil OR butter substitute

1 cup organic cane sugar

2 tsp. vanilla

3 egg whites

⅓ cup vanilla rice, nut or seed milk

Dry Ingredients

1¼ cup whole grain sorghum flour

1¼ cup whole grain brown rice flour

½ cup sweet rice flour

1 tsp. cream of tartar

1 tsp. baking soda

1 tsp. baking powder

2 tsp. xanthan gum

½ tsp. salt

PREHEAT OVEN TO 350°F.

1. In a stand mixer, combine wet ingredients. In a separate bowl, whisk dry ingredients together and add to wet ingredients. Mix until incorporated.

2. Roll out dough on an oiled baking sheet. Cut into shapes with cookie cutters and remove excess dough. (Or, place dough in a cookie press and press on to an oiled baking sheet. Decorate with sprinkles before baking.)

3. Bake 7-9 minutes for small pressed cookies, 12-15 minutes for larger cookie-cutter cookies. Watch carefully so they don't get too brown.

4. Ice with frosting (if desired) after baking.

Nutritional Information Per Serving
Servings 48 ✳ Calories 74 ✳ Fat 3g ✳ Protein 1g ✳ Carbohydrates 12g ✳ Cholesterol 0mg ✳ Sodium 63mg ✳ Fiber 0g

ALTERNATIVE COOK, LLC™

JAMMIE SAMMIES

A pretty cookie to give as a gift, or to make for your Valentine. One cookie is plenty because they are BIG! These freeze well in individual-serving reclosable bags.

Ingredients

1 jar strawberry Just Fruit® preserves
2 TBS organic cane sugar

PREHEAT OVEN TO 350°F.

1. Make a batch of the **Sugar Cookie** dough (Page 104) and refrigerate 2 hours.

2. Oil hands and baking surface and roll out dough about ½" thick. Using a heart-shaped or round, fluted-edge cookie cutter (4½ x 3½"), cut dough for the bottoms. Using a smaller heart, or round cookie cutter (3 x 2"), cut out the center of the tops. Carefully remove the dough around the cutouts. Generously sprinkle sugar on both the bottoms and tops.

3. Bake 10 to 12 minutes. Cool.

4. Thickly smear the bottom cookie with your favorite fruit preserves and place the "cut out" cookie on top to make a "sandwich."

Nutritional Information Per Serving
Servings 12 ✳ Calories 295 ✳ Fat 10g ✳
Protein 3g ✳ Carbohydrates 48g ✳ Cholesterol 0mg ✳
Sodium 254mg ✳ Fiber 2g

SNICKERDOODLES

These cinnamony, sweet, tender cookies are a hit with kids. And so easy and fast to make anytime.

Ingredients
2 tsp. cinnamon
2 TBS organic cane sugar

PREHEAT OVEN TO 350°F.

1. Make one recipe of the **Sugar Cookies** (Page 104). (For a more 'buttery' taste, use butter substitute instead of oil.)

2. Place cinnamon and sugar into a bowl.

3. Roll cookie dough into 2" balls and roll the balls in the cinnamon and sugar. Place on an oiled baking sheet and for 10 to 12 minutes.

Nutritional Information Per Serving
Servings 24 ✳ Calories 155 ✳ Fat 5g ✳ Protein 2g ✳
Carbohydrates 26g ✳ Cholesterol 0mg ✳
Sodium 127mg ✳ Fiber 1g

LEMON "ZESTIES" (VEGAN)

Lemon oil makes these thin, crisp cookies taste "deep with lemon." You'll have the best results if the dough is allowed to rest and chill a few hours before baking.

Wet Ingredients

¼ cup walnut or sunflower oil

½ cup agave nectar

2 tsp. vanilla

1 tsp. liquid lecithin

½ tsp. lemon oil (or a few drops, depending on the taste and oil pungency)

Dry Ingredients

½ cup whole grain sorghum flour

¼ cup whole grain brown rice flour

2 TBS arrowroot

1 TBS lemon zest *

⅛ tsp. baking powder

Tiny pinch of salt

PREHEAT OVEN TO 350°F
(After the dough has chilled.)

1. In a food processor, emulsify the wet ingredients. Add the dry ingredients and process until incorporated. Wrap dough in plastic and chill for 2 hours in the refrigerator.

2. Use 1 tsp. of dough per cookie, placed three across on a Silpat. (These cookies spread out a lot.)

3. Bake 12 minutes.

Use just the yellow part of the rind, not the white pith, which is bitter.

Nutritional Information Per Serving
Servings 24 ✳ Calories 61 ✳ Fat 3g ✳ Protein 0g ✳
Carbohydrates 10g ✳ Cholesterol 0mg ✳
Sodium 11mg ✳ Fiber 0g

VANILLA THINS (VEGAN)

This is a super-versatile cookie! It is good alone, yet can be made into a chocolate sandwich cookie. The baked cookies work well as a pie crust base for a sweet pie. Another recipe you'll turn to again and again.

Wet Ingredients
¼ cup walnut or sunflower oil
½ cup agave nectar
½ tsp. vanilla powder* or vanilla
1 tsp. liquid lecithin

Dry Ingredients
½ cup whole grain sorghum flour
¼ cup amaranth flour, toasted
2 TBS cornstarch
2 TBS almond meal
⅛ tsp. baking powder
¼ tsp. salt

PREHEAT OVEN TO 350°F.

1. In a food processor, emulsify the wet ingredients.

2. Toast the amaranth flour in a dry pan on the stovetop. This enhances its flavor. Toast flour by placing it in a dry sauce pan and heating and stirring until aromatic.

3. Add the dry ingredients to the food processor and pulse until incorporated. Wrap dough in plastic and refrigerate 2 hours.

4. Oil hands and drop circles of the dough on a Silpat. Use about 1 TBS dough per cookie. These will spread when they bake. Bake 12 minutes.

*The vanilla powder emulsifies the oil as well as adding a rich vanilla taste to the cookie.

Nutritional Information Per Serving
Servings 24 ✳ Calories 66 ✳ Fat 3g ✳ Protein 1g ✳
Carbohydrates 10g ✳ Cholesterol 0mg ✳
Sodium 34mg ✳ Fiber 0g

CHOCOLATE SANDWICHES (VEGAN)

A thin vanilla cookie with exquisite chocolate sandwiched in the middle. These cookies remind me of a popular packaged cookie. Choose your favorite chocolate bar for these cookies.

Ingredients
1 recipe **Vanilla Thins**
4 oz. GFCF dark chocolate bar

1. Make one recipe **Vanilla Thins** (Page 108), shaping cookies into ovals.

2. Chop chocolate on a cutting board. Place in a double boiler and melt. Dip the bottom of one cookie in the chocolate and "sandwich" with another cookie. Let sandwiches cool to harden chocolate.

Nutritional Information Per Serving
Servings 12 ✳ Calories 177 ✳ Fat 8g ✳ Protein 2g ✳
Carbohydrates 26g ✳ Cholesterol 0mg ✳
Sodium 69mg ✳ Fiber 1g

CHOCOLATE CHIP COOKIES (VEGAN)

My husband and I sometimes play one of my favorite imagination games: "If you only had 3 foods to eat, what would they be?" Where the rules of the game include considering taste, satiation and sustainability. These cookies are always top on my list — and by the way, it's OK to be "heavy handed" with the chocolate chips!

Flax Mix
⅓ cup water
1 TBS whole flax seeds

Wet Ingredients
½ cup sunflower oil
1 tsp. liquid lecithin

Dry Ingredients
¾ cup gafava, garbanzo or soy flour
¾ cup tapioca flour
¾ cup whole grain sorghum flour
½ cup Sucanat®
½ cup organic cane sugar
1½ tsp. xanthan gum
¾ tsp. baking soda
½ tsp. salt

2 tsp. vanilla
¾ cup GFCF chocolate chips
¼ cup water

PREHEAT OVEN TO 350°F.

1. Place flax seeds and water into a blender and process until smooth. Transfer Flax Mix (there should be about ¼ cup) to a stand mixer, add oil and lecithin and emulsify until incorporated.

2. In a separate bowl, whisk the dry ingredients together.

3. Combine dry ingredients with wet ingredients. Let dough rest 5 minutes.

4. Oil hands and form dough into 2" balls. Bake on a Silpat 22-24 minutes.

Nutritional Information Per Serving
Servings 24 ✳ Calories 154 ✳ Fat 8g ✳ Protein 2g ✳
Carbohydrates 20g ✳ Cholesterol 0mg ✳
Sodium 87mg ✳ Fiber 1g

ALTERNATIVE COOK, LLC™

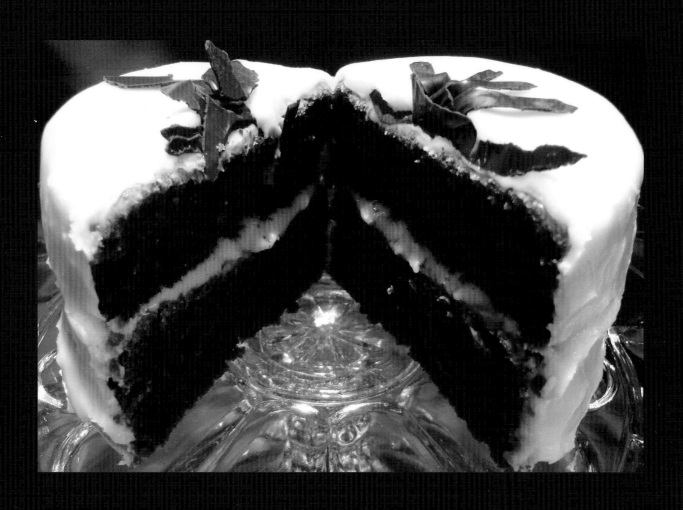

Red Velvet Cake with White Icing, Page 40
Strawberry Soufflés, Page 86

From top left: Light, White Sandwich Bread, Page 151
Orange Cream Pie, Page 198, Focaccia, Page 156
Yellow Layered Cake with Raspberry Filling, Page 46
Almond Apricot Bundt Cake, Page 44, Baked Custard, Page 97

Above: French Bread, Page 152

Opposite page, from top left:
Cheesecake, Page 50
Cherry Crisp, Page 202
Upside Down Coffee Cake with Whipped Topping, Page 178
Glazed Apple Sticky Buns, Page 180
Chocolate, Chocolate Chip Angel Food Cake, Page 55
Cinnamon Raisin Bread, Page 142

Above: Berry Cream Tarts with Peach Glaze, Page 195

Opposite page, from top left:
Oatmeal Raisin Cookies, Page 102
Angel Food Cake, Page 54
Peanut Butter / Chocolate Chip Bars, Page 77
Ladyfingers, Page 98
Cranberry Walnut Bread, Page 134

Chinese Almond Cookies, Page 120
Pumpkin Pudding Squares, Pages 201

"BROWN SUGAR" COOKIES

These puffy, brown-sugar tasting cookies are a perfect lunchbox treat. They are made with Sucanat®, a more wholesome, delicious brown sugar substitute.

Wet Ingredients

2 cups Sucanat® or brown sugar
1 cup walnut or sunflower oil
4 egg whites
2 tsp. vanilla

Dry Ingredients

1½ cups whole grain sorghum flour
1 cup whole grain brown rice flour
¾ cup cornstarch
1 tsp. baking soda
¼ tsp. salt

PREHEAT OVEN TO 350°F.

1. In a stand mixer, combine wet ingredients.

2. Add dry ingredients and mix until incorporated. Let dough sit 5 minutes.

3. Oil hands and form dough into 2" sized balls and place on a Silpat or oiled baking sheet. Flatten slightly, to about ½" thickness. Bake 12-14 minutes, until barely done.

Nutritional Information Per Serving
Servings 24 ✳ Calories 203 ✳ Fat 10g ✳ Protein 2g ✳
Carbohydrates 28g ✳ Cholesterol 0mg ✳
Sodium 90mg ✳ Fiber 1g

CHOCOLATE COOKIES (VEGAN)

This recipe produces a chewy, tasty chocolate cookie that is great by itself or can be used in various other ways. Fill with marshmallow cream, a nut butter or Rice Dream® ice cream and voilà! A special treat! A comparison of the recipe using xylitol in place of cane sugar follows.

Flax Mix
⅓ cup water
1 TBS whole flax seeds

Wet Ingredients
½ cup sunflower oil
1 tsp. liquid lecithin
2 tsp. vanilla

Dry Ingredients
¾ cup whole grain sorghum flour
¼ cup gafava, garbanzo or soy flour
¾ cup tapioca flour
½ cup cocoa powder
1 cup organic cane sugar or xylitol
1½ tsp. xanthan gum
1 tsp. baking soda
½ tsp. salt

¼ cup water

PREHEAT OVEN TO 350°F.

1. Combine flax seeds and water in a blender and process until smooth.

2. Emulsify the wet ingredients and the Flax Mix in a stand mixer until incorporated.

3. In a separate bowl, whisk the dry ingredients together.

4. Combine dry ingredients with wet; add water. Let mixture sit 5 minutes.

5. Oil hands and form into 2" sized balls. Bake on a Silpat or oiled cookie sheet 20-24 minutes.

Nutritional Information Per Serving
With sugar:
Servings 24 ✳ Calories 111 ✳ Fat 5g ✳ Protein 1g ✳
Carbohydrates 16g ✳ Cholesterol 0mg ✳
Sodium 98mg ✳ Fiber 1g
With xylitol:
Servings 24 ✳ Calories 83 ✳ Fat 5g ✳ Protein 1g ✳
Carbohydrates 9g ✳ Cholesterol 0mg ✳
Sodium 98mg ✳ Fiber 1g

ALTERNATIVE COOK, LLC™

COMPARISON:
CHOCOLATE COOKIES

ORGANIC CANE SUGAR
versus
XYLITOL

The recipe was followed exactly the same except in one batch organic cane sugar was used, and in the other, xylitol was used. Cookies were baked on a Silpat. The same size dough-balls were made, along with using the same pan, oven, and oven temperature.

Organic Cane Sugar Cookie

✷ Would present this to company

✷ Tastes great

✷ Has a nice texture (more cookie-like), crisp on the outside and chewy on the inside

✷ 4" diameter cookie

Xylitol Cookie

✷ Passable for an at-home treat; would not present this cookie to company

✷ "Something was missing" on initial taste, and it had a sweet after-taste.

✷ "Rubbery" texture

✷ 3" diameter cookie

Clearly, the crystals in the organic cane sugar result in a better textured cookie, as well as a satisfying sweet taste. But, I'm not ruling out the xylitol cookie. Xylitol is an important sweetener for diabetics, for those following a yeast-reducing diet and for those following a low-glycemic diet.

RUSSIAN TEA CAKES (VEGAN)

Many cultures around the world have a version of this cookie. Finally, here's a gluten-free, dairy-free, leavening-free, egg-free version we can enjoy with reckless abandon!

Wet Ingredients

1 cup butter substitute

½ cup confectioner's sugar

2 tsp. guar gum

2 tsp. vanilla

Dry Ingredients

1 cup whole grain sorghum flour

1 cup whole grain brown rice flour

¼ cup cornstarch, Expandex™, tapioca flour or arrowroot

¼ tsp. salt

1 cup chopped pecans

1 cup confectioner's sugar for dusting

PREHEAT OVEN TO 325°F.

1. Cream wet ingredients with a hand mixer.

2. In a separate bowl, whisk dry ingredients together, then add to wet and mix thoroughly.

3. Form dough into 2" sized balls or small half moons on a Silpat or an oiled baking sheet. Bake 19 minutes.

4. Place confectioner's sugar in a closable plastic bag. Remove baked cookies from the oven and place a few directly into the bag. Shake gently to coat with the sugar. Remove from bag and cool on a wire rack. Place in bag with confectioner's sugar and coat again.

Nutritional Information Per Serving

Servings 24 ✳ Calories 165 ✳ Fat 11g ✳
Protein 1g ✳ Carbohydrates 16g ✳ Cholesterol 0mg ✳
Sodium 112mg ✳ Fiber 1g

PECAN SANDIES

A little salty, a little sweet, "buttery" and easy to make. These disappear quickly!

Dry Ingredients

½ cup whole grain sorghum flour
½ cup whole grain brown rice flour
½ cup Expandex™, cornstarch,
 tapioca flour or arrowroot
½ tsp. xanthan gum
1 tsp. salt
½ cup organic cane sugar

Wet Ingredients

½ cup butter substitute
½ cup chopped pecans
¼ cup water
1 tsp. baking powder
½ tsp. baking soda
1 tsp. vanilla

18-24 whole pecans

PREHEAT OVEN TO 375°F.

1. Whisk dry ingredients together in a bowl. Add wet ingredients to the bowl and mix with a pastry whisk.

2. Roll out dough about ½" thick and cut into 2" squares. Press a whole pecan on top. Bake on a Silpat 14-15 minutes.

Nutritional Information Per Serving
Servings 24 ✳ Calories 114 ✳ Fat 7g ✳ Protein 1g ✳
Carbohydrates 13g ✳ Cholesterol 0mg ✳
Sodium 181mg ✳ Fiber 1g

"GINGERBIRDS" / GINGERSNAPS

The aroma of ginger cookies baking in the oven is heavenly. We started a tradition in our home, cutting the dough into the shape of penguins, calling them "Gingerbirds" and hanging them on the Christmas tree. Mesquite flour (available online) adds a wonderful "woody" taste. If you can't find it, substitute whole grain brown rice flour. The whole grain teff flour contributes protein and a rich, beautiful color.

Wet Ingredients

½ cup walnut oil

½ cup Sucanat®

1 egg white

1 tsp. liquid lecithin

½ cup molasses

1 TBS apple cider vinegar

1 tsp. guar gum

Dry Ingredients

1¼ cup whole grain sorghum flour

¼ cup mesquite flour OR whole grain brown rice flour

⅓ cup whole grain teff flour

¼ cup cornstarch, tapioca flour or arrowroot

¼ cup white bean flour

1 tsp. xanthan gum

1 tsp. baking soda

1½ tsp. ground ginger

½ tsp. cinnamon

½ tsp. cloves

PREHEAT OVEN TO 375°F.

1. In a stand mixer, emulsify wet ingredients. In a separate bowl, whisk dry ingredients together. Combine dry ingredients with wet ingredients in the mixer. Cover mixer bowl with plastic wrap and chill dough for 1 hour.

2. Roll out dough to ⅛" thickness on a Silpat or an oiled baking sheet. Cut into shapes with a cookie cutter. Peel away excess dough. If making into ornaments, poke a hole with a ⅛" dowel to put ribbon through when baked.

3. Bake 6 minutes. Decorate with **White Icing**, (Page 41).

Nutritional Information Per Serving

Servings 36 ✳ Calories 81 ✳ Fat 4g ✳ Protein 1g ✳ Carbohydrates 12g ✳ Cholesterol 0mg ✳ Sodium 40mg ✳ Fiber 1g

MERINGUE COOKIES

Light and airy, high-protein, no fat and only 14 calories per cookie — there are few reasons not to eat these crunchy, blissful "bite-fulls." These cookies resemble the kind sold in European bakeries and use the same baking technique. If you like, you can pipe these into "baskets" and fill them with fresh berries.

Ingredients
4 egg whites
½ cup organic cane sugar
½ tsp. cream of tartar
1 tsp. vanilla

PREHEAT OVEN TO 175°F.

1. Place egg whites in a metal or glass bowl and beat until foamy. Add cream of tartar and gradually add sugar, one TBS at a time, until glossy, stiff peaks form. Fold in vanilla.

2. Place mixture into a piping bag and pipe into desired shapes on a Silpat, parchment paper, or other baking surface.

3. Bake 3 hours or until crunchy. (When they come off the pan without sticking, they are done.) Turn oven off and let cookies cool in the oven. (They will crisp up as they cool.)

Nutritional Information Per Serving
Servings 32 ✳ Calories 14 ✳ Fat 0g ✳ Protein 0g ✳ Carbohydrates 3g ✳ Cholesterol 0mg ✳ Sodium 7mg ✳ Fiber 0g

HAZELNUT MERINGUE COOKIES

Enjoy the kiss of nutty chocolate that hazelnut brings. This meringue cookie uses a different technique than the previous one. This one "bakes" whereas the Meringue Cookie "dries."

Nut Mixture

1 cup whole, raw hazelnuts
¼ cup cocoa powder

Meringues

4 egg whites
1 cup organic cane sugar
½ tsp. cream of tartar
1 tsp. vanilla

PREHEAT OVEN TO 350°F.

1. Toast hazelnuts according to the directions on Page 210. Remove from oven and cool. Place nuts in a food processor and process into a fine powder. Add cocoa powder and pulse until incorporated.

2. In a metal or glass bowl beat egg whites until foamy. Add cream of tartar. Beat until stiff and shiny, adding sugar a little at a time. Add vanilla.

3. Fold in nut mixture. Place into a piping bag and pipe "kisses" on a Silpat, parchment paper or another baking surface. Bake 15-20 minutes. Turn oven off and leave cookies in the oven until the oven is cold. Serve.

Nutritional Information Per Serving

Servings 32 ✳ Calories 53 ✳ Fat 3g ✳ Protein 1g ✳
Carbohydrates 7g ✳ Cholesterol 0mg ✳
Sodium 0mg ✳ Fiber 0g

CHINESE ALMOND COOKIES (VEGAN)

These are the perfect finish to a Chinese-themed meal. Decorate with slivered almonds on top.

Wet Ingredients

6 raw cashews or hemp seeds

⅓ cup + 1 TBS water

⅓ cup walnut or sunflower oil

2 tsp. vanilla

1 tsp. lemon juice

1 TBS fresh lemon zest or ½ tsp. dried

⅛ tsp. freshly ground nutmeg

2 TBS butter substitute

1 tsp. almond extract

Dry Ingredients

½ cup whole grain sorghum flour

¼ cup tapioca flour

½ cup gafava, soy or garbanzo bean flour

¼ cup potato starch

¼ tsp. salt

1½ tsp. baking powder

½ tsp. baking soda

⅓ cup organic cane sugar (Reserve 1 TBS for sprinkling tops)

Slivered or blanched almonds to decorate the tops

PREHEAT OVEN TO 425°.

1. Place wet ingredients in a blender and blend until smooth.

2. In a separate bowl, whisk dry ingredients together.

3. Add the wet ingredients to the dry ingredients and mix by hand with a flat whisk until incorporated. Do not over mix.

4. Roll out dough on an oiled baking surface and cut into rounds. Place on a Silpat or oiled baking sheet 1" apart. Sprinkle tops with organic cane sugar.

5. Bake 10-12 minutes or until golden brown. Remove from baking sheet and place on a rack until cooled. Serve immediately or cool and store in an airtight container.

Nutritional Information Per Serving
Servings 24 ✳ Calories 84 ✳ Fat 5g ✳ Protein 1g ✳
Carbohydrates 9g ✳ Cholesterol 0mg ✳
Sodium 91mg ✳ Fiber 0g

ALTERNATIVE COOK, LLC™

PINWHEELS (VEGAN)

A fun, fast recipe to make with leftover pie crust. Or use the entire pie crust recipe for a whole batch of pinwheels! These are best served warm, straight from the oven. Yum!

Ingredients

1 recipe **Perfect Pie Crust** (Page 209)

¼ cup organic cane sugar

2 tsp. cinnamon

¼ cup finely chopped walnuts (optional)*

¼ cup chopped currants (optional)*

PREHEAT OVEN TO 350°F.

1. Roll dough on waxed paper into a rectangle or square about ¼" thick. Sprinkle with sugar, cinnamon, nuts and currants. Roll up tightly, and cut into ½" thick slices.

2. Place on a baking sheet and bake 10-15 minutes. Transfer to a wire rack to cool.

Experiment with other combinations of nuts and dried fruits. Try finely chopped dates or cranberries and walnuts, dried apricots or cherries with almonds.

Nutritional Information Per Serving
Servings 32 ✳ Calories 59 ✳ Fat 3g ✳ Protein 1g ✳
Carbohydrates 7g ✳ Cholesterol 0mg ✳
Sodium 34mg ✳ Fiber 0g

CHOCOLATE DREAMS

Unleash your creative spirit with this recipe! Put the batter into a cake decorator tube and make any shape you like! Stars, squiggles, rosettes or chocolate ropes – the fun is in the crunch!

Wet Ingredients

6 eggs whites

½ tsp. cream of tartar

¾ cup organic cane sugar
 OR ¼ tsp. stevia

2 tsp. vanilla

Dry Ingredients

¼ cup whole grain sorghum flour

¼ cup whole grain brown rice flour

¼ cup cornstarch

¼ cup cocoa powder

1½ tsp. xanthan gum

1 tsp. baking powder

Tiny pinch of salt

PREHEAT OVEN TO 400°F.

1. Prepare a baking sheet with a Silpat or parchment paper.

2. With the whisk attachment, beat the egg whites until foamy. Add cream of tartar and the organic cane sugar a little at a time, or stevia and beat until stiff peaks form.

3. In a separate bowl, whisk dry together ingredients.

4. Carefully, fold dry ingredients into the egg whites being careful not to over mix.

5. Place mixture into a cake decorator and pipe into shapes on parchment or on a Silpat. Bake on 12-15 minutes.

Nutritional Information Per Serving

With sugar:

Servings 32 ✳ Calories 31 ✳ Fat 0g ✳ Protein 1g ✳ Carbohydrates 7g ✳ Cholesterol 0mg ✳ Sodium 26mg ✳ Fiber 0g

With stevia:

Servings 16 ✳ Calories 31 ✳ Fat 0g ✳ Protein 1g ✳ Carbohydrates 5g ✳ Cholesterol 0mg ✳ Sodium 52mg ✳ Fiber 0g

COMPARISON:
CHOCOLATE DREAMS

STEVIA
versus
ORGANIC CANE SUGAR

The recipe was followed exactly the same except in one batch stevia was used, and in the other, organic cane sugar was used. Cookies were baked on a Silpat.

Stevia Cookie *(top)*

❋ Darker color

❋ Less expansive (recipe made about half as many cookies)

❋ Not as pleasant taste, a little bitter after-taste

❋ Passable for a high protein "for the family" snack; would not serve these to company

Organic Cane Sugar Cookie

❋ Nice color and texture

❋ Expansive, light, crunchy cookie

❋ Pleasant taste

❋ Would serve these to company

Both versions were fast and easy to make, but the recipe using cane sugar turns out a nicer cookie.

Muffins and Quick Breads

Muffins and quick breads are easy and delicious. They can be sweet or savory, eaten for breakfast or a snack. A basket of freshly made muffins is a perfect hostess gift and a warm way to welcome a new family to the neighborhood. And, who doesn't love receiving a brightly wrapped loaf of your special quick bread at the holidays? No one needs to know how easy they are to make! All they'll notice is how appetizing they taste!

Many of these recipes use less sugar than their traditional counterparts, instead incorporating fruits or vegetables such as pumpkin and carrots to enhance not just taste, but nutritional content.

BLUEBERRY BUCKLE MUFFINS

*Warm blueberry muffins right out of the oven — ah, how homey and satisfying.
These delectable bites are made even better with the addition of a delicious topping.
For me, the Buckle is the best part and sometimes I double it in this recipe! I prefer
to use dried blueberries because of their concentrated taste, plus fresh or frozen
blueberries add more moisture and can throw off the recipe proportions.*

Wet Ingredients

½ cup rice, nut or seed milk

½ cup sparkling water

¼ cup sunflower oil

2 egg whites

½ cup organic cane sugar

½ tsp. apple cider vinegar

Dry Ingredients

1 cup whole grain sorghum flour

¾ cup whole grain brown rice flour

¼ cup amaranth flour

2 tsp. baking powder

½ tsp. salt

¾ cup dried blueberries

Buckle

½ cup slivered almonds

¼ cup organic cane sugar

1 tsp. cinnamon

3 TBS walnut or sunflower oil

PREHEAT OVEN TO 400°F.

1. Combine wet ingredients in a bowl. Mix together until sugar is dissolved.

2. Separately, whisk dry ingredients together.

3. Add dry ingredients to wet ingredients and mix until incorporated.

4. Pour batter into an oiled muffin pan and fill to the top of each muffin cup. Let batter sit a few minutes to allow flours to absorb the moisture. Mix Buckle in a bowl and sprinkle on the top of each muffin.

5. Bake 25 minutes. Cover with parchment paper after baking 10 minutes to keep the buckle from over-browning.

Nutritional Information Per Serving
Servings 9 ✳ Calories 401 ✳ Fat 16g ✳ Protein 6g ✳
Carbohydrates 59g ✳ Cholesterol 0mg ✳
Sodium 248mg ✳ Fiber 4g

ALTERNATIVE COOK, LLC™

GINGERBREAD MUFFINS

Ginger, molasses, cinnamon all combined into a richly spiced, flavorsome muffin. The teff flour makes these a beautiful color and adds a pleasing depth of taste. This is a favorite in my home.

Wet Ingredients

¼ cup molasses

½ cup rice, nut or seed milk

½ cup sparkling water

¼ cup sunflower oil

2 egg whites

½ cup Sucanat®

1 tsp. ginger

1 tsp. cinnamon

½ tsp. apple cider vinegar

Dry Ingredients

¾ cup whole grain teff flour

¾ cup whole grain sorghum flour

½ cup whole grain brown rice flour

2 tsp. baking powder

½ tsp. salt

1 TBS ground flax meal

PREHEAT OVEN TO 350°F.

1. Combine wet ingredients in a bowl. Mix together until sugar is dissolved.

2. Separately, whisk dry ingredients together. Add dry ingredients to wet ingredients.

3. Pour batter into an oiled muffin pan and fill to the top of each muffin cup. Let batter sit a few minutes to allow flours to absorb the moisture. Bake 25 minutes.

Nutritional Information Per Serving
Servings 10 ✳ Calories 243 ✳ Fat 8g ✳ Protein 5g ✳
Carbohydrates 39g ✳ Cholesterol 0mg ✳
Sodium 26mg ✳ Fiber 4g

CARROT RAISIN MUFFINS (VEGAN)

These are a great after-school or after work snack. The heavenly aroma will jump start your taste buds even before these moist muffins are out of the oven!

Flax Mix
2 TBS flax seeds
⅔ cup water

Wet Ingredients
½ cup Sucanat®
⅓ cup Nayonaise® (or other mayonnaise)
⅓ cup walnut or sunflower oil
1 cup shredded carrots
½ cup raisins
½ cup apple juice concentrate
½ cup chopped dried apples
2 tsp. vanilla
½ cup pecans, chopped
½ cup organic cane sugar

Dry Ingredients
½ cup whole grain sorghum flour
½ cup whole grain brown rice flour
½ cup tapioca flour
1 tsp. cinnamon
1 tsp. xanthan gum
1½ tsp. baking powder
¼ tsp. salt

PREHEAT OVEN TO 350°F.

1. Soak raisins in apple juice concentrate until plump, then drain excess apple juice.

2. In a blender, process flax seed and water until smooth. Place in a bowl and add the other wet ingredients.

3. In a separate bowl, whisk dry ingredients together. Add the dry ingredients to the wet ingredients and mix until incorporated.

4. Pour batter into an oiled muffin pan and fill to the top of each muffin cup. Let batter sit a few minutes to allow flours to absorb the moisture. Bake 45 minutes, covering with parchment after 20 minutes to prevent over-browning.

Nutritional Information Per Serving
Servings 9 ✳ Calories 398 ✳ Fat 20g ✳ Protein 3g ✳
Carbohydrates 55g ✳ Cholesterol 0mg ✳
Sodium 195mg ✳ Fiber 2g

BANANA MUFFINS (VEGAN)

Super quick and super easy — all you need is a bowl and a blender! In no time at all, you can be eating wholesome homemade muffins. I love these muffins! Sucanat® is a great tasting sugar to pair with bananas.

Flax Mix
1 tsp. flax seed
1½ TBS water

Wet Ingredients
¼ cup sunflower or walnut oil
1 tsp. vanilla
3 ripe bananas
¼ cup sparkling water

Dry Ingredients
1 cup whole grain sorghum flour
¼ cup whole grain brown rice flour
¼ cup tapioca flour
¼ cup almond meal
1½ tsp. baking powder
⅛ tsp. salt
½ cup Sucanat®

PREHEAT OVEN TO 350°F.

1. In a blender, combine flax seed and water. Blend until smooth. Add wet ingredients. Blend until smooth.

2. In a separate bowl, whisk dry ingredients together. Add to blender. Blend until smooth.

3. Pour batter into an oiled muffin pan* and fill to the top of each muffin cup. Let batter sit a few minutes to allow flours to absorb the moisture. Bake 27-29 minutes.

The batter can also be made into a loaf (8 x 4.5" pan); bake 40-45 minutes.

Nutritional Information Per Serving
Servings 9 ✳ Calories 231 ✳ Fat 8g ✳ Protein 4g ✳
Carbohydrates 38g ✳ Cholesterol 0mg ✳
Sodium 117mg ✳ Fiber 2g

CORNBREAD MUFFINS

The sweet taste of corn works so well as a muffin or quick bread. Eat these the "southern way", sliced in half and slathered with honey or molasses. Or, go south of the border and give them a Mexican flare by adding some chopped green chilies or jalapenos, a little chili powder and a pinch of cumin.

Wet Ingredients

¼ cup honey or agave nectar

½ cup rice, nut or seed milk

½ cup sparkling water

¼ cup sunflower oil

2 egg whites

Dry Ingredients

1¼ cups rice flour

¾ cup yellow corn meal

2 tsp. baking powder

½ tsp. salt

PREHEAT OVEN TO 400°F.

1. Mix wet ingredients in a bowl.

2. In a separate bowl, mix dry ingredients. Add the dry ingredients to the wet ingredients and whisk until blended.

3. Pour batter into an oiled muffin pan and fill to the top of each muffin cup. Let batter sit a few minutes to allow flours to absorb the moisture. Bake 25 minutes.

Nutritional Information Per Serving

Servings 9 ✻ Calories 215 ✻ Fat 7 g ✻ Protein 3g ✻ Carbohydrates 35g ✻ Cholesterol 0mg ✻ Sodium 232mg ✻ Fiber 2g

CONFETTI CORNBREAD MUFFINS

Get a little sneaky! Adding ground dehydrated vegetables into your cornbread adds nutrition and a surprising look. Dehydrate your own veggies, or use a product called Just Veggies®.

Wet Ingredients

2 TBS agave nectar

½ cup rice, nut or seed milk

½ cup sparkling water

¼ cup sunflower oil

2 egg whites

Dry Ingredients

¾ cup whole grain brown rice flour

¾ cup whole grain corn meal

½ cup ground dehydrated vegetables (measure before grinding in a food processor to a coarse powder)

2 tsp. baking powder

1 tsp. garlic salt

PREHEAT OVEN TO 400°F.

1. Whisk wet ingredients in a bowl.

2. In a separate bowl, mix dry ingredients. Add the dry ingredients to the wet and whisk until blended.

3. Pour batter into an oiled muffin pan and fill to the top of each muffin cup. Or, batter can be placed into an oiled 9" square pan for cornbread. Let batter sit a few minutes to allow flours to absorb the moisture. Bake 25 minutes.

Nutritional Information Per Serving

Servings 9 ✳ Calories 241 ✳ Fat 7g ✳ Protein 4g ✳ Carbohydrates 41g ✳ Cholesterol 0 mg ✳ Sodium 470mg ✳ Fiber 3g

TEFF MUFFINS WITH HERBS

Teff is an ancient grain, its use dating back to the time of the Egyptian pyramids. It is also the smallest grain in the world; 150 grains of teff equal the weight of one grain of wheat. Teff is versatile and packed with protein. These savory muffins pair nicely with soup and salad.

Wet Ingredients

2 TBS blackstrap molasses
½ cup rice, nut or seed milk
¾ cup sparkling water
¼ cup sunflower oil
2 egg whites
½ tsp. apple cider vinegar

Dry Ingredients

¾ cup whole grain teff flour
¾ cup whole grain sorghum flour
½ cup whole grain brown rice flour
2 tsp. baking powder
1 tsp. onion powder
½ tsp. garlic powder
½ tsp. dried basil
½ tsp. ground rosemary
½ tsp. salt
2 TBS ground flax meal

PREHEAT OVEN TO 400°F.

1. Combine wet ingredients in a bowl.

2. Separately, whisk dry ingredients together. Add dry ingredients to wet ingredients.

3. Pour batter into an oiled muffin pan and fill to the top of each muffin cup. Let batter sit a few minutes to allow flours to absorb the moisture. Bake 25 minutes.

Nutritional Information Per Serving
Servings 9 ✳ Calories 228 ✳ Fat 9g ✳ Protein 5g ✳
Carbohydrates 33g ✳ Cholesterol 0mg ✳
Sodium 238mg ✳ Fiber 4g

ALTERNATIVE COOK, LLC™

ZESTY DINNER MUFFINS (VEGAN)

Try these dinner muffins as an alternative to yeast rolls. These have an Italian flare, but feel free to experiment with different herb combinations to compliment your dinner entrée.

Flax Mix

1 TBS flax seeds
⅓ cup water
1 clove garlic
1 tsp. dried basil

Wet Ingredients

1 tsp. apple cider vinegar
¼ cup sunflower
1 tsp. agave nectar
2 cups sparkling water
¼ cup chopped black olives
2 TBS chopped dried tomatoes (packed in oil/drained)
1 TBS hemp seed (optional)

Dry Ingredients

1 cup whole grain sorghum flour
⅔ cup gafava bean flour
½ cup tapioca flour
2 tsp. xanthan gum
1½ tsp. garlic salt
1 tsp. baking soda
2 tsp. baking powder

PREHEAT OVEN TO 350°F.

1. In a blender, process Flax Mix until smooth. Whisk wet ingredients and Flax Mix together in a bowl.

2. In a separate bowl, whisk dry ingredients together. Combine dry ingredients with wet ingredients and whisk until incorporated.

3. Pour batter into an oiled muffin pan and fill to the top of each muffin cup. Smooth the tops with an oiled finger and let batter sit a few minutes to allow flours to absorb the moisture. Bake 25-30 minutes. Turn out on a rack to cool.

Nutritional Information Per Serving
Servings 12 ✳ Calories 104 ✳ Fat 2g ✳ Protein 3g ✳ Carbohydrates 18g ✳ Cholesterol 0mg ✳ Sodium 215mg ✳ Fiber 2g

CRANBERRY WALNUT BREAD

Dried cranberries (usually sweetened) packed with vitamin C and antioxidants are available all year long so you can bake this quick bread as often as you like! If you can find them, dried cranberries infused with orange are wonderful in this recipe.

Wet Ingredients

2 egg whites
⅓ cup walnut oil
2 tsp. vanilla
½ cup plain, gluten-free soy yogurt
⅓ cup rice, nut or seed milk

Dry Ingredients

¾ cup whole grain sorghum flour
¼ cup whole grain brown rice flour
¼ cup tapioca flour
½ cup Sucanat®
1½ tsp. baking powder
½ tsp. baking soda
1 tsp. xanthan gum
⅔ cup dried cranberries
½ cup chopped walnuts
1 tsp. cinnamon
¼ tsp. fresh ground nutmeg
¼ tsp. salt

PREHEAT OVEN TO 350°F.

1. Beat wet ingredients together.

2. In a separate bowl, whisk dry ingredients together. Combine dry ingredients with wet ingredients.

3. Place batter into an oiled 8½ x 4½" loaf pan. Let sit a few minutes to allow flours to absorb moisture. Bake 45 minutes, covering with parchment paper after 20 minutes to prevent over-browning. Remove from oven and turn out on a rack to cool.

Nutritional Information Per Serving
Servings 12 ✳ Calories 193 ✳ Fat 10g ✳
Protein 4g ✳ Carbohydrates 24g ✳ Cholesterol 0mg ✳
Sodium 177mg ✳ Fiber 1g

PUMPKIN SPICE BREAD

The sublime aroma of pumpkin and spices always takes my thoughts back to past holiday dinners with family and loved ones. Pumpkin bread is a favorite and freezes well — make a batch in little bread pans and keep on hand for a quick hostess gift. This bread is the perfect mid-afternoon snack with a cup of coffee or tea. A vegan version follows, with a comparison of the two on Page 137.

Wet Ingredients

4 egg whites
¼ cup walnut or sunflower oil
1 tsp. vanilla
1 cup canned pumpkin
¼ cup sparkling water

Dry Ingredients

1 cup whole grain sorghum flour
¼ cup whole grain brown rice flour
¼ cup tapioca flour
¼ cup almond meal
2 tsp. baking powder
⅛ tsp. salt
½ cup Sucanat®
¼ cup organic cane sugar
1 tsp. cinnamon
1 tsp. ground ginger
¼ tsp. freshly ground nutmeg
¼ tsp. cloves
1 tsp. xanthan gum

PREHEAT OVEN TO 350°F.

1. In a bowl, whisk wet ingredients together.

2. In a separate bowl, whisk dry ingredients together. Add dry ingredients to wet ingredients. Whisk until incorporated.

3. Place batter into an oiled 8½ x 4½" loaf pan. Let batter sit a few minutes to allow flours to absorb moisture. Bake 35-45 minutes, covering with parchment paper after 20 minutes to prevent over-browning. Remove from oven and turn out on a wire rack to cool.

Nutritional Information Per Serving
Servings 12 ✳ Calories 174 ✳ Fat 6g ✳ Protein 4g ✳
Carbohydrates 28g ✳ Cholesterol 0mg ✳
Sodium 127mg ✳ Fiber 1g

PUMPKIN SPICE BREAD (VEGAN)

Using soy protein isolate and flax meal in place of egg whites slightly affects the texture of this bread, but doesn't change the scrumptious flavor one bit!

Flax Mix
1 TBS flax seed
⅓ cup water

Wet Ingredients
4 tsp. soy protein isolate powder
½ cup plus 2 TBS sparkling water
¼ cup walnut or sunflower oil
1 tsp. vanilla
1 cup canned pumpkin

Dry Ingredients
1 cup whole grain sorghum flour
¼ cup whole grain brown rice flour
¼ cup tapioca flour
¼ cup almond meal
2 tsp. baking powder
⅛ tsp. salt
½ cup Sucanat®
¼ cup organic cane sugar
1 tsp. cinnamon
1 tsp. ground ginger
¼ tsp. freshly ground nutmeg
¼ tsp. cloves
1 tsp. xanthan gum

PREHEAT OVEN TO 350°F.

1. In a blender, combine flax seed and water. Blend until smooth. Add wet ingredients. Blend until smooth.

2. In a separate bowl, whisk dry ingredients together. Add to blender, and process until smooth.

3. Place batter into an oiled 8½ x 4½" baking pan. Let batter sit a few minutes to allow flours to absorb moisture. Bake 35-45 minutes covering with parchment after 20 minutes to prevent over-browning. Remove from oven and turn out on a rack to cool.

Nutritional Information Per Serving
Servings 12 ✳ Calories 175 ✳ Fat 6g ✳ Protein 4g ✳
Carbohydrates 29g ✳ Cholesterol 0mg ✳
Sodium 110mg ✳ Fiber 2g

COMPARISON:
PUMPKIN SPICE BREAD

EGG WHITES
versus
SOY PROTEIN ISOLATE

The recipe was followed exactly the same, except in one, egg whites were used and in the other, soy protein isolate was used. Loaves were baked in the same oven, using the same pan at the same temperature.

The Egg White Loaf	**The Soy Protein Isolate Loaf**
✳ Great taste	✳ Great taste
✳ Nice texture / crumb	✳ Passable texture, crumb (a little denser)
✳ Rose well, moist bread	✳ Rose less than egg-white loaf, moist bread
✳ Pleasing color	✳ Pleasing color
✳ Would serve this to company	✳ Would serve this to company

Both loaves were good, respectable and virtually interchangeable. The loaf made with egg whites had a lighter texture.

LEMON POPPY SEED BREAD

This moist lemony bread is a nice change of pace. It has a wonderful texture and delicious taste combination of sweet and tart.

Wet Ingredients

½ cup organic cane sugar

⅓ cup walnut or sunflower oil

2 egg whites

2 tsp. lemon zest

1 tsp. lemon oil (or a few drops, depending on the taste and oil pungency)

3 tsp. lemon juice

⅓ cup rice, nut or seed milk

½ cup plain yogurt*

Dry Ingredients

¾ cup whole grain sorghum flour

¼ cup whole grain brown rice flour

¼ cup sweet rice flour

1 TBS poppy seeds

1 tsp. baking powder

½ tsp. baking soda

PREHEAT OVEN TO 350°F.

1. Beat wet ingredients together.

2. In a separate bowl, whisk dry ingredients together. Combine dry ingredients with wet ingredients.

3. Place batter into an oiled 8½ x 4½" baking pan. Let batter sit a few minutes to allow flours to absorb moisture. Bake 45 minutes. Remove from oven and turn out on a rack to cool before slicing.

Soy, or any kind you choose.

Nutritional Information Per Serving
Servings 12 ✳ Calories 166 ✳ Fat 7g ✳ Protein 2g ✳
Carbohydrates 24g ✳ Cholesterol 0mg ✳
Sodium 111mg ✳ Fiber 1g

ALTERNATIVE COOK, LLC™

Breads, Buns, Pizza and Focaccia

Bread is truly the staff of life. It's a staple at most meals: toast for breakfast, a sandwich for lunch, rolls for dinner. And pizza – one of the best foods of all time! Living a GFCF lifestyle does not mean you have to give up your favorite breads – or eat the highly refined off-the-shelf gluten-free breads you find in the food stores.

A variety of breads are featured in this section, all emphasizing whole grain flours except one, for the "white bread" lover in your home. And, please don't be daunted by the number of ingredients in some of these recipes. Just measure out "mixes" of the combined dry ingredients into individual bags, marked with the page number in this cookbook and pop them into the freezer. Whenever you need to bake a loaf, remove one of the bags, mix with the wet ingredients and you're good to go. It saves a ton of time, and makes bread-making fast!

CINNAMON RAISIN BREAD

This is one of my favorite breads. It's wonderful toasted for breakfast, makes a **Fantastic French Toast** *(Page 191), and I use it often for sandwiches with a nut or seed butter. Leftover slices are perfect in bread pudding…that's if you ever have any leftovers! This recipe uses an oven-rising technique. The oven is a warm, air-tight place, perfect to allow bread dough to rise properly.*

Wet Ingredients
¼ cup sunflower oil
4 egg whites
1 tsp. vanilla

Dry Ingredients
½ cup whole grain sorghum flour
¼ cup whole grain teff flour
¾ cup potato starch
½ cup arrowroot
¼ cup potato flour
¾ cup tapioca flour or cornstarch
½ cup Sucanat® or brown sugar
1 tsp. salt
1 tsp. xanthan gum
½ tsp. guar gum
2 tsp. cinnamon
1 cup raisins

Yeast Mixture
1½ cups warm water
2 tsp. yeast

PREHEAT OVEN TO 375°F
(After the bread rises and is ready to bake.)

1. Heat the oven to 175° and turn it off. Mix yeast and warm water in a measuring cup. Let stand for 5 minutes until foamy. Using a hand mixer, beat egg whites in a bowl until foamy. Add vanilla, oil and yeast mixture. Beat.

2. In a separate bowl, whisk dry ingredients together (except raisins). Add dry ingredients to wet ingredients along with the yeast mixture and beat together with a mixer for 1 minute until incorporated. Add raisins.

3. Pour batter into an oiled 9 x 5" loaf pan and oil hands to shape loaf into a dome. Place into the warmed oven to rise. When the loaf has doubled in size, carefully remove from the oven, preheat the oven to 375° and place the loaf back into the oven to bake. Bake 65-75 minutes. Cover after 30 minutes to prevent over-browning. Remove from baking pan and place on a rack to cool. Slice and serve.

Nutritional Information Per Serving
Servings 12 ✳ Calories 233 ✳ Fat 5g ✳ Protein 3g ✳
Carbohydrates 45g ✳ Cholesterol 0mg ✳
Sodium 181mg ✳ Fiber 2g

NO YEAST MONTINA® SANDWICH BREAD

This is a fast and easy light-textured bread that's a staple in my house. It is especially appealing to someone avoiding yeast. I love the taste of Montina® flour, but if you can't find it, use buckwheat flour. Nutritionists always emphasize incorporating a wide variety of foods into our diet — this bread is composed of a variety of flours. Plus, it freezes well.

Wet Ingredients
5 egg whites
1½ cups rice, nut or seed milk
2 TBS sunflower oil
⅛ tsp. stevia OR 3 TBS sugar

Dry Ingredients
½ cup tapioca flour
½ cup arrowroot flour
½ cup gafava flour (or garbanzo, soy, or fava bean)
½ cup sorghum flour
½ cup white bean, navy bean or white rice flour
¼ cup potato starch
¼ cup Montina® flour or buckwheat flour
1 tsp. xanthan gum
1 tsp. salt
1 tsp. baking soda
1 tsp. baking powder
½ tsp. cream of tartar

PREHEAT OVEN TO 375°F.

1. Mix wet ingredients in a mixing bowl with an electric mixer.

2. In a separate bowl, whisk dry ingredients together. Add to wet ingredients and mix until incorporated.

3. Place into an oiled 8½ x 4½" loaf pan and bake 65-70 minutes, covering with parchment paper after 30 minutes to prevent over-browning. Turn out on a wire rack to cool.

Nutritional Information Per Serving
Servings 12 ✳ Calories 160 ✳ Fat 4g ✳ Protein 5g ✳ Carbohydrates 26g ✳ Cholesterol 0mg ✳ Sodium 360mg ✳ Fiber 1g

NO YEAST WHOLE GRAIN BUNS (VEGAN)

Shape these versatile buns into any size that fits your need, from small to super-sized! Cut in half and smear on your favorite jelly for a nice breakfast.

Flax Mix

1 TBS whole flax seeds

⅓ cup water

Wet Ingredients

2 tsp. xanthan gum

1 tsp. apple cider vinegar

¼ cup sunflower or safflower oil

⅓ cup powdered rice or soy milk

1 tsp. liquid lecithin (optional)

1 tsp. salt

1 tsp. agar powder

1 TBS agave nectar

1 tsp. baking soda

2 tsp. baking powder

1 cup sparkling water

Dry Ingredients

½ cup whole grain sorghum flour

½ cup white bean flour (or any bean flour)

½ cup Montina® flour or buckwheat flour

½ cup tapioca flour

PREHEAT OVEN TO 375°F.

1. In a blender, emulsify flax seeds and water. Remove Flax Mix from blender and place in a food processor fit with the cutting blade. Add wet ingredients. Process 30 seconds until thick.

2. Add dry ingredients and process 30 seconds.

3. Place a cookie sheet with ½" of water on the oven floor, or on a lower rack. Oil hands and shape dough into buns. Bake on a Silpat or other baking surface 20-25 minutes until the bottom sounds hollow when tapped. Remove to a wire rack to cool.

Nutritional Information Per Serving
Servings 12 ✳ Calories 142 ✳ Fat 7g ✳ Protein 3g ✳
Carbohydrates 17g ✳ Cholesterol 0mg ✳
Sodium 253mg ✳ Fiber 1g

EVERYDAY WHOLE GRAIN BREAD

Make this bread once and I'm sure you'll agree that this is the best whole-grain bread! It has a great taste and a good chewy texture. After it's made, slice it and freeze two pieces in sandwich-size reclosable bags for quick sandwiches.

Wet Ingredients

Small Loaf	Full Size Loaf
2	4 egg whites
2 TBS	¼ cup walnut or sunflower oil
½ tsp.	1 tsp. apple cider vinegar
½ tsp.	1 tsp. liquid lecithin (optional)
½ tsp.	1 tsp. agar powder
½ tsp.	1 tsp. guar gum

Yeast Mixture

Small Loaf	Full Size Loaf
¾ cup+2 TBS	1¾ cups sparkling water, warmed (105°-110°)
1 TBS	1 TBS + 1 tsp. yeast (Do not double for full-size loaf.)

Dry Ingredients

Small Loaf	Full Size Loaf
¼ cup+2 TBS	¾ cup buckwheat flour
¼ cup	½ cup garbanzo or gafava bean flour
¼ cup	½ cup whole grain sorghum flour
¼ cup	½ cup whole grain teff flour
¼ cup	½ cup potato starch
2 TBS	¼ cup almond meal
1 TBS	2 TBS Expandex™, cornstarch, tapioca flour or arrowroot
¼ tsp. + ⅛ tsp.	¾ tsp. lecithin granules (optional)
1 TBS	2 TBS cocoa powder
1 tsp.	2 tsp. organic cane sugar
1 tsp.	2 tsp. xanthan gum
½ tsp.	1 tsp. salt
1½ tsp.	1 TBS flax meal
1½ tsp.	1 TBS toasted sesame seeds
1½ tsp.	1 TBS toasted sunflower seeds

PREHEAT OVEN TO 375°F
(After the bread rises and is ready to bake.)

1. Place a cookie sheet with ½" of water in it on the oven floor. Heat the oven to 175° and turn it off. (Bread rises best between 80-85°F.)

2. Dry roast sesame and sunflower seeds in a dry frying pan on the stove over high heat. Keep them moving and roast until browned (a few minutes).

3. Using a stand mixer, beat egg whites until foamy. Add other wet ingredients and mix until combined.

4. In a mixing cup combine warm water with yeast and let sit 5 minutes until foamy. In a separate bowl, whisk dry ingredients together.

5. Add the yeast mixture with all dry ingredients into the mixer bowl containing the wet ingredients. Mix 30 seconds. For small loaf, place batter in an oiled 8½ x 4½" loaf pan. For the large loaf, use a 9 x 5" loaf pan. Place the bread in the cooling oven to rise until doubled in size. Remove from oven carefully. Remove pan with water from oven.

6. Increase heat to 375°F. When oven is preheated, put bread back into oven and bake 65-75 minutes for the large loaf and about 55-60 minutes for the small loaf. (Do not under-bake.) Place parchment paper over the top after the first 20 minutes to prevent over-browning. Remove bread from pan and tap the bottom. It should sound hollow. If not, bake 5-10 minutes longer (covered with parchment). Turn out onto a wire rack and cool completely.

Nutritional Information Per Serving

Servings 12 ✳ Calories 201 ✳ Fat 8g ✳ Protein 7g ✳
Carbohydrates 26g ✳ Cholesterol 0mg ✳
Sodium 180mg ✳ Fiber 4g

EVERYDAY WHOLE GRAIN BREAD (VEGAN)

This is a vegan adaptation which uses soy protein isolate powder instead of egg whites and liquid soy lecithin as a dough enhancer. A comparison of the two versions follows this recipe.

Flax Mix

1 TBS flax seeds

⅓ cup water

Wet Ingredients

Small Loaf	Full Size Loaf
2 TBS	¼ cup soy protein isolate powder
¼ cup	½ cup water
2 TBS	¼ cup of the Flax Mix (above)
2 TBS	¼ cup of walnut or sunflower oil
½ tsp.	1 tsp. apple cider vinegar
½ tsp.	1 tsp. liquid lecithin (optional)
½ tsp.	1 tsp. agar powder
½ tsp.	1 tsp. guar gum

Yeast Mixture

Small Loaf	Full Size Loaf
1 cup	2 cups sparkling water warmed (110°)
2½ tsp.	2½ tsp. yeast (Do not double for full-size loaf.)

Dry Ingredients

Small Loaf	Full Size Loaf
¼ cup +2 TBS	¾ cup buckwheat flour
¼ cup	½ cup whole grain gafava or garbanzo bean flour
¼ cup	½ cup whole grain sorghum flour
¼ cup	½ cup whole grain teff flour
¼ cup	½ cup potato starch
2 TBS	¼ cup almond meal
1 TBS	2 TBS Expandex™, cornstarch, tapioca flour or arrowroot
¼ tsp.+ ⅛ tsp.	¾ tsp. lecithin granules
1 TBS	2 TBS cocoa powder
1 tsp.	2 tsp. organic cane sugar
1 tsp.	2 tsp. xanthan gum
½ tsp.	1 tsp. salt
1½ tsp.	1 TBS toasted sesame seeds
1½ tsp.	1 TBS toasted sunflower seeds

PREHEAT OVEN TO 375°F
(After the bread rises and is ready to bake.)

1. Place a cookie sheet with ½" of water in it on the floor of the oven. Heat oven to 175° and turn it off. (Bread rises best between 80-85°F.)

2. Dry roast sesame and sunflower seeds together in a dry frying pan on the stove over high heat. Keep them moving and roast until browned (a few minutes).

3. Using a stand mixer, beat soy protein isolate and water until foamy. Then add other wet ingredients and mix until combined.

4. In a mixing cup combine warm water with yeast and let sit 5 minutes until foamy. In a separate bowl, whisk dry ingredients together.

5. Add the yeast mixture with all dry ingredients into the mixer bowl containing the wet ingredients. Mix 30 seconds. For small loaf, place batter in an oiled 8½ x 4½" loaf pan. For the large loaf, use a 9 x 5" loaf pan. Place the bread in the cooling oven to rise until doubled in size. Remove from oven carefully. Remove pan with water from oven.

6. Increase heat to 375°F. When oven is preheated, put bread back into oven and bake 65-75 minutes for the large loaf and about 55-60 minutes for the small loaf. (Do not under-bake.) Place parchment paper over the top after the first 20 minutes to prevent over-browning. Remove bread from pan and tap the bottom. It should sound hollow. If not, bake 5-10 minutes longer (covered in parchment). Turn out onto a wire rack and cool completely.

Nutritional Information Per Serving

Servings 12 ✳ Calories 207 ✳ Fat 10g ✳
Protein 7g ✳ Carbohydrates 28g v Cholesterol 0mg ✳
Sodium 165mg ✳ Fiber 4g

COMPARISON:
EVERYDAY WHOLE GRAIN BREAD

SOY PROTEIN ISOLATE
versus
EGG WHITES

The recipe was followed exactly the same, except soy protein isolate was used in one loaf, and egg whites were used in the other. Loaves were baked in the same size pan, using the same oven at the same temperature.

The Soy Protein Isolate Loaf

* Nice taste

* Nice texture / crumb

* Rose above the pan before baking and contracted a little while baking

The Egg White Loaf

* Nice taste

* Nice texture / crumb

* Rose above the pan before baking and contracted some (but less than the soy protein isolate loaf) while baking

Both loaves are good, respectable and virtually interchangeable. The loaf made with egg whites expanded more and has a slightly lighter texture. Either recipe makes good everyday bread.

LIGHT, WHITE SANDWICH BREAD

This recipe is sure to please the white bread lover in your home. It makes nice, chewy-crusted bread with a soft interior. Plus, it's fast and easy to make — especially if you assemble batches of the dry ingredients ahead of time.

Yeast Mixture

1 cup water
2 tsp. yeast

Wet Ingredients

1 cup sparkling water
3 egg whites
3 TBS sunflower oil
1 tsp. rice vinegar
½ tsp. guar gum

Dry Ingredients

½ cup sorghum flour
¾ cup tapioca flour
1 TBS potato flour
½ cup arrowroot, cornstarch or potato starch
½ cup white rice flour
3 TBS organic cane sugar
½ tsp. xanthan gum
1 tsp. salt

PREHEAT OVEN TO 375°F.

1. In a measuring cup, heat water to 105° and then add yeast. Let it sit until foamy. Mix the wet ingredients in a mixing bowl for 2 minutes on high speed.

2. In a separate bowl, whisk the dry ingredients together. Add the dry ingredients to the mixing bowl, and add the yeast mixture. Mix until incorporated, about 1 minute on high speed.

3. Pour batter into an oiled 9 x 5" loaf pan and cover with plastic wrap. Let it rise in a warm place until doubled in size. Carefully remove the plastic wrap. Place dough in a preheated oven and bake 60-70 minutes. (Do not under bake.) Place parchment paper over loaf after 20 minutes of baking to prevent over-browning. Turn out onto a wire rack to cool.

Nutritional Information Per Serving
Servings 12 ✳ Calories 154 ✳ Fat 4g ✳ Protein 2g ✳
Carbohydrates 28g ✳ Cholesterol 0mg ✳
Sodium 195mg ✳ Fiber 1g

FRENCH BREAD

Crusty on the outside, chewy on the inside. French bread is known by its texture, taste and characteristic long loaf shape. If you happen to have a French bread pan lying around the kitchen, great! It makes those authentic-looking marks on the bottom of the loaf, and helps it to hold its shape while baking. If not, loaves can be baked on a piece of parchment paper on a baking sheet, or in a pan with sides.

Yeast Mixture
2 TBS yeast
1 cup warm water

Dry Ingredients
1 cup whole grain brown rice flour
½ cup whole grain sorghum flour
½ cup potato starch
½ cup Expandex™, tapioca flour, cornstarch or arrowroot
2 tsp. salt
2 tsp. xanthan gum
1 tsp. guar gum
2 tsp. lecithin granules

Wet Ingredients
3 egg whites
¼ cup organic cane sugar
¼ cup rice, nut or seed milk
1 tsp. agar powder
2 tsp. rice vinegar

PREHEAT OVEN TO 450°F.

1. Place dry ingredients in a bowl and whisk until incorporated. In a measuring cup, add yeast to warm water and let sit until yeast proofs (until foamy).

2. In a separate bowl, beat egg whites until foamy. Add other wet ingredients and the yeast mixture. Add dry ingredients to wet ingredients and mix with a hand mixer a few minutes.

3. Oil hands and divide dough into 2 parts, then place on an oiled surface and shape into a loaf. (The dough is sticky, and oiling your hands enables you to form and smooth the loaf.) Carefully place in a French bread pan, or other pan. Slash the loaf three times diagonally with a sharp knife. Cover with plastic wrap. Let rise until doubled in size.

4. Remove plastic wrap and bake loaves 25-30 minutes, covering with parchment paper to prevent over-browning. The bottom of the loaves should sound hollow when thumped. Turn out onto a wire rack to cool. Makes 2 loaves.

Nutritional Information Per Serving
Servings 12 ✳ Calories 125 ✳ Fat 1g ✳ Protein 3g ✳
Carbohydrates 26g ✳ Cholesterol 0mg ✳
Sodium 374mg ✳ Fiber 2g

COMPARISON:
FRENCH BREAD

TAPIOCA FLOUR
versus
EXPANDEX™

The recipe was followed exactly the same except in one tapioca flour was used and in the other Expandex™ was used. Loaves were baked in a French bread pan.

The Tapioca Flour Loaf

✳ Would present this loaf to company

✳ Tasted good; familiar French bread taste

✳ Had a little denser texture/crumb than the Expandex™ loaf

The Expandex™ Loaf

✳ Would present this loaf to company

✳ Tasted good; familiar French bread taste

✳ Had a lighter more "French bread" texture (more air-bubbles)

Either loaf was acceptable. Expandex™ gave the loaf a "lighter" texture - more similar to conventional French bread.

GF "RYE" BREAD (VEGAN)

As a child I remember always wanting to buy the "party rye" bread at the deli — those tiny square thinly sliced dark breads were so appealing to a little one like me. As an adult, I still love the taste of rye bread but it's so difficult to find a true GF version. But, since the "rye" taste comes from the caraway seeds, and the bread's richness from cocoa powder, this recipe will satisfy the child or adult in you! This recipe also illustrates a different rising technique for breads.

Dry Ingredients
1 cup whole grain sorghum flour
½ cup whole grain teff flour
¼ cup cocoa powder
¼ cup white bean or navy bean flour
½ cup Expandex™, cornstarch, tapioca flour or arrowroot
1 tsp. garlic salt
½ tsp. onion powder
½ tsp. caraway seeds
½ tsp. ground celery seed
1 tsp. xanthan gum
1 TBS + 1 tsp. yeast

Wet Ingredients
2 cups warm water
1 tsp. apple cider vinegar

PREHEAT OVEN TO 375°F
(After the bread rises and is ready to bake.)

1. In a bowl, whisk dry ingredients together. Using a hand mixer, mix in wet ingredients for about 2 minutes, until incorporated. Place dough into two oiled 5½ x 3" mini loaf pans. Oil hands and pat the top of the dough to smooth.

2. Place loaf pans in a soup pot (or plastic sealable container) and cover with a lid. (This provides an air-tight place for the dough to rise.) Place in a warm location and let dough rise until doubled in size. Remove baking pans from container.

3. Transfer to preheated oven and bake 45-55 minutes, covering with parchment after baking 30 minutes to prevent over-browning. Bake until the loaf sounds hollow when tapped on the bottom. Turn out onto a wire rack to cool.

Nutritional Information Per Serving
Servings 12 ✳ Calories 115 ✳ Fat 2g ✳ Protein 4g ✳
Carbohydrates 22g ✳ Cholesterol 0mg ✳
Sodium 175mg ✳ Fiber 3g

ALTERNATIVE COOK, LLC™

PIZZA

Homemade pizza is the best, and making it can be almost as much fun as eating it! Gather guests together and offer an array of toppings using this easy, yet delicious pizza crust. Use any kind of pan you have – a pizza pan, cookie sheet, or baking pan all work!

Wet Ingredients

1 Pizza	2 Pizzas
1½ cups + 2 TBS	3¼ cups warm water
2 TBS	¼ cup olive oil
½ tsp.	1 tsp. agar powder or flakes
1½ tsp.	1 TBS yeast
1½ tsp.	1 TBS honey

Dry Ingredients

1 Pizza	2 Pizzas
¾ cup	1½ cups sorghum flour
½ cup	1 cup brown rice flour
¼ cup	½ cup potato flour
¼ cup	½ cup tapioca flour
¼ cup	½ cup arrowroot or cornstarch
½ tsp.	1 tsp. salt
2 TBS	¼ cup ground flax seed
½ tsp.	1 tsp. xanthan gum
½ tsp.	1 tsp. guar gum

PREHEAT OVEN TO 425°F.

1. In a measuring cup, dissolve agar powder and yeast in warm water. In a mixing bowl, combine other wet ingredients.

2. In a separate mixing bowl, whisk dry ingredients until incorporated. Add dry ingredients and the yeast mixture to wet ingredients and mix with a hand-held electric mixer 2-3 minutes.

3. Press dough into pan with oiled hands until it is about ½" thick. Prick entire dough with a fork and let it rise 20 minutes. (I like using an 8 x 8" pan.)

4. Pre-bake crust for 10 minutes. Remove from the oven and top with your favorite pizza toppings. Bake 20 additional minutes.

Note: If topping a pizza with vegetables such as zucchini, peppers, mushrooms, eggplant and onions: slice vegetables ½" thick, spray with spray-on oil, lightly salt and pre-bake at 425° for 25-30 minutes. Place them, along with sauce and other toppings on the pre-baked crust, and bake pizza for the remaining time.

Nutritional Information Per Serving
Servings 12 ✳ Calories 260 ✳ Fat 8g ✳ Protein 4g ✳ Carbohydrates 44g ✳ Cholesterol 0mg ✳ Sodium 184mg ✳ Fiber 4g

FOCACCIA

What's the difference between pizza and focaccia? Focaccia is usually thicker, and is topped with olive oil and herbs. This bread has a lovely taste and texture. Focaccia makes wonderful sandwich bread and is great in paninis! This recipe can also be used as a pizza crust.

Wet Ingredients

1 Focaccia	2 Focaccia
¼ cup + 2 TBS	¾ cup warm water
¼ tsp.	½ tsp. agar powder
1½ tsp.	1 TBS olive oil
¼ tsp.	½ tsp. cider vinegar
1 tsp.	2 tsp. guar gum
1½ tsp.	1 TBS yeast

Dry Ingredients

1 Focaccia	2 Focaccia
½ cup + 2 TBS	1¼ cups whole grain sorghum flour
½ cup	1 cup whole grain brown rice flour
¼ cup	½ cup tapioca flour
¼ cup	½ cup arrowroot or potato starch
2 TBS	¼ cup ground flax seeds
½ tsp.	1 tsp. salt
½ tsp.	1 tsp. dried oregano and dried basil
½ cup	1 cup water

Kosher salt, sun dried tomatoes packed in oil, fresh basil, or what ever you desire (on top)

PREHEAT OVEN TO 425°F.

1. In a measuring cup, dissolve agar powder in warm water. Add other wet ingredients and yeast. (This will make a gel-like substance.) Set aside.

2. In a separate mixing bowl, whisk dry ingredients (except water) until incorporated. Add wet ingredients to dry ingredients and mix with a hand-held electric mixer for 1 minute. Add remaining water.

3. Oil hands and form dough into a ball. Roll out dough on an oiled pizza pan until it is about ½" thick. Let it rise in a warm place 30 minutes, or until it doubles in height. Top with chopped sun-dried tomatoes packed in oil (drained) and sprinkle with kosher salt.

4. Bake 15 minutes. Add fresh herbs and bake 5 more minutes. Serve immediately.

Nutritional Information Per Serving
Servings 8 ✳ Calories 266 ✳ Fat 5g ✳ Protein 5g ✳ Carbohydrates 51g ✳ Cholesterol 0mg ✳ Sodium 242mg ✳ Fiber 4g

CROUTONS

Anytime I make bread, I tuck a few slices away in the freezer to use as bread crumbs or to make into croutons. Croutons add that extra "something" to a salad or soup and they are so easy to make.

Ingredients
3-4 slices of bread
Spray on olive oil
Garlic salt

PREHEAT OVEN TO 350°F.

1. Spray a baking sheet with spray-on olive oil. Cube bread and place on baking sheet. Spray the top with spray-on oil. Sprinkle with garlic salt.

2. Place in an oven and bake 10-15 minutes until crisp. Cool and serve. These freeze well.

Nutritional Information Per Serving
Servings 4 ✳ Calories 160 ✳ Fat 4g ✳ Protein 5g ✳ Carbohydrates 26g ✳ Cholesterol 0mg ✳ Sodium 360mg ✳ Fiber 1g

Snacks

A crisp cracker, a crunchy breadstick, a handful of pretzels or nuts — ah, don't we all love snacks? These recipes will restore your faith that you can enjoy crunchy, delicious treats. Even better — most are quick and easy to make!

ITALIAN "CHEESE" CRACKERS

Why buy the expensive GFCF brands from the store or online sources when you can whip up these crackers in no time? Once you've made a batch, I think you'll agree: there is nothing better than a warm cracker straight from the oven.

Dry Ingredients

½ cup whole grain sorghum flour

½ cup white or navy bean flour

¼ cup tapioca flour

¼ cup cornstarch

1 tsp. xanthan gum

½ tsp. salt

1 tsp. organic cane sugar

Wet Ingredients

5 oz. GFCF mozzarella style "cheese"

½ cup sun-dried tomatoes (packed in herbs and oil)

1 tsp. apple cider vinegar

2 tsp. each: dried oregano, dried basil, dried marjoram

2 TBS olive oil

¼ cup water

Kosher salt to sprinkle on top

PREHEAT OVEN TO 375°F.

1. Whisk dry ingredients together in a bowl. Drain and chop sun-dried tomatoes. Add wet ingredients to dry and mix until incorporated.

2. Make little balls and flatten with the bottom of a glass, or roll out dough to about ¼" thick. Dock dough. Cut out with a cookie cutter, or simply cut dough into squares. Sprinkle with kosher salt. Bake on a Silpat or an oiled cookie sheet for 15 minutes. Transfer crackers to a wire rack to cool.

Note: Docking is simply pricking the dough all over. It is an important step in making crackers, because the little holes make the crackers lighter. You can dock with a fork, or find a docking tool at your local kitchen store.

Nutritional Information Per Serving
Servings 24 ✳ Calories 50 ✳ Fat 2g ✳ Protein 2g ✳
Carbohydrates 8g ✳ Cholesterol 0mg ✳
Sodium 92mg ✳ Fiber 0g

BREADSTICKS

Breadsticks — you probably thought you'd never see these again when converting to a gluten-free diet. Breadsticks are fun to make and addicting to eat. These are just delicious — crunchy on the outside and soft on the inside. Bake these to serve right out of the oven with your next Italian-style dinner.

Yeast Mixture
½ cup water
1 tsp. yeast

Wet Ingredients
½ cup water
1 egg white
2 TBS sunflower oil
½ tsp. rice vinegar
¼ tsp guar gum

Dry Ingredients
¼ cup whole grain sorghum flour
¼ cup tapioca flour
2 TBS potato flour
½ cup arrowroot, cornstarch or potato starch
¼ white rice flour
1 TBS organic cane sugar
¼ tsp. xanthan gum
½ tsp. salt

PREHEAT OVEN TO 425°F.

1. In a measuring cup, heat water to 105° and then add yeast. Let it sit until foamy. Mix the other wet ingredients in a mixing bowl for 1 minute on high speed.

2. In a separate bowl, whisk dry ingredients until incorporated. Add dry ingredients and yeast mixture to "wet" mixing bowl and mix 1 minute on high speed.

3. Place batter in a pastry bag without a tip and pipe sticks 10-12" long and ½" thick on a Silpat or an oiled cookie sheet. Let sticks rise in a warm place 30-45 minutes. Bake 15-20 minutes until golden brown. Cool on Silpat or baking surface. Best if eaten the same day as baked, but these will keep in an air-tight container.

Note: If you do not have a pastry bag, simply place the batter in a plastic bag and cut off a corner.

Nutritional Information Per Serving
Servings 32 ✳ Calories 43 ✳ Fat 1g ✳ Protein 0g ✳
Carbohydrates 8g ✳ Cholesterol 0mg ✳
Sodium 51mg ✳ Fiber 0g

SOCCA / GARBANZO BEAN CRACKERS

Socca are popular as an afternoon snack in the Mediterranean, where they are usually cooked in a big copper pan, then broken apart and eaten. Socca is a thin cracker with just a few basic ingredients – garbanzo bean flour, olive oil, water and salt, with black pepper added to taste. Since most of us don't have a big copper pan in our kitchens, this is a baked version. The garbanzo bean flour lends an earthy flavor to the cracker, accented nicely by the bite of the black pepper.

Ingredients
1 cup water
2 TBS olive oil
1 cup garbanzo flour
¾ tsp. salt
½ tsp. black pepper (to taste)

PREHEAT OVEN TO 400°F.

1. In a blender, process ingredients for 1 minute, scraping the sides as necessary. The batter will be thin.

2. Spread batter onto a Silpat or oiled baking sheet and bake 12-15 minutes until browned. Cool on Silpat or baking sheet until crisp. (Makes two large crackers to be broken and served.)

3. These are best when served right from the oven.

Nutritional Information Per Serving
Servings 16 ✳ Calories 38 ✳ Fat 3g ✳ Protein 2g ✳
Carbohydrates 2g ✳ Cholesterol 0mg ✳
Sodium 67mg ✳ Fiber 1g

ALTERNATIVE COOK, LLC™

VEGETABLE CRACKERS

Just Veggies® are dehydrated mixed vegetables and are widely available now in grocery stores. Dehydrated soup vegetables are almost the same (they usually contain onion) and can be found in the bulk food section. (It is important to check with the store to ensure their bulk section is gluten-free). Either work well in this recipe.

Ingredients

1 cup dehydrated vegetables
1 cup whole grain sorghum flour
½ cup whole grain brown rice flour
¼ cup olive oil
2 tsp. xanthan gum
½ cup water
½ tsp. salt

Kosher salt (for topping)

PREHEAT OVEN TO 400°F.

1. In a food processor, process dehydrated vegetables. You should have about ½ cup of "vegetable flour" after processing 1 cup of dehydrated vegetables.

2. Add the rest of the ingredients to the food processor and pulse until a ball forms.

3. Oil hands, baking sheet and rolling pin. Roll dough out on a baking sheet to ¼" thickness and cut out shapes with a cookie cutter. Peel away excess dough.

4. Dock crackers either by poking holes in them with a fork or by using a docking tool. Top with kosher salt.

5. Bake 10-12 minutes. These crackers get crispy as they cool, and are best eaten the same day they are baked.

Nutritional Information Per Serving
Servings 48 ✳ Calories 33 ✳ Fat 1g ✳ Protein 1g ✳
Carbohydrates 5g ✳ Cholesterol 0mg ✳
Sodium 26mg ✳ Fiber 1g

RICE CRACKERS

This is an innovative, delicious way to use left-over rice! Next time you eat at a Chinese restaurant, bring home the extra rice and make these treasures!

Ingredients

2 cups (day-old) cooked white or brown rice
2 TBS olive oil
1 TBS lime juice
½ tsp. garlic salt
½ tsp. garlic powder

PREHEAT OVEN TO 400°F.

1. Process ingredients in a food processor until a smooth paste forms. Taste and adjust garlic salt according to preference.

2. Oil baking sheet or use a Silpat. Oil rolling pin and fingers. Pat paste into a ball on the baking surface and roll out until it is ¼" thick. Cut into shapes.

3. Bake 20-25 minutes. These are best when served right from the oven.

Nutritional Information Per Serving
Servings 36 ✳ Calories 45 ✳ Fat 1g ✳ Protein 1g ✳
Carbohydrates 8g ✳ Cholesterol 0mg ✳
Sodium 29mg ✳ Fiber 0g

MEXICAN CHILI FLAX CRACKERS

Flax seeds are thought to be extremely healthy, containing all 9 essential amino acids. They are one of the best sources of omega 3 fatty acids and are packed with protein. These crispy crackers are a powerhouse of flavor and nutritional value.

Ingredients

1 cup whole flax seeds

½ cup raw almonds, walnuts or sunflower seeds

¼ cup nutritional yeast

1 tsp. garlic salt

1 tsp. chili powder

1 tsp. ground cumin

Kosher salt for topping

PREHEAT OVEN TO 400°F.

1. Soak flax seeds in water for 3 hours and drain excess water but do not rinse.

2. Combine all ingredients in a food processor and process for a few minutes until a sticky dough forms.

3. On a Silpat or an oiled baking sheet, form 1" balls and press with the bottom of an oiled glass until flat (about 2½" diameter and ⅛" thick). Dock by poking holes in the crackers with a fork or rolling with a docking tool.

4. Sprinkle with a little kosher salt to taste. Bake 10-12 minutes. Cool on Silpat or baking surface until crisp.

Nutritional Information Per Serving
Servings 24 ✻ Calories 55 ✻ Fat 4g ✻ Protein 3g ✻ Carbohydrates 4g ✻ Cholesterol 0mg ✻ Sodium 46mg ✻ Fiber 2g

"CHEDDAR CHEESE" CRACKERS

For people who can't eat gluten and dairy, a good "cheese" cracker is hard to find. No longer! I am thrilled with the Follow Your Heart brand of "cheeses." They are dairy and gluten-free, they melt and taste great! Ume plum vinegar adds zing to these crackers.

Ingredients

¼ cup water

¼ cup whole grain sorghum flour

¼ cup whole grain brown rice flour

¼ cup cornstarch, tapioca flour or arrowroot

⅔ cup shredded soy cheddar cheese*

1 TBS nutritional yeast

3 TBS olive oil

1 TBS ume plum vinegar

¼ tsp. salt

PREHEAT OVEN TO 375°F.

1. Mix ingredients together in a bowl by hand until ingredients are incorporated.

2. Form mixture into a disk and wrap in plastic. Chill 2 hours.

3. Roll out dough to ¼" thickness on a Silpat or oiled baking sheet. With a plastic knife (to avoid damaging the Silpat), cut into 1" squares. Dock crackers either by poking holes with a fork or rolling with a docking tool.

4. Bake 15-17 minutes, until browned. Be careful not to over-bake. Cool on Silpat or baking surface until crisp.

*Note: Please make sure the cheese substitute package specifies "casein free" – not all "cheese" substitutes are!

Nutritional Information Per Serving

Servings 24 ✳ Calories 45 ✳ Fat 3g ✳ Protein 1g ✳ Carbohydrates 4g ✳ Cholesterol 0mg ✳ Sodium 109mg ✳ Fiber 0g

NO SOY "CHEESE" CRACKERS

These thin, crisp crackers are surprisingly good, especially when served warm from the oven. They are reminiscent of the flavor of a cheese cracker but made without the cheese!

Ingredients

¼ cup water
¼ cup whole grain sorghum flour
¼ cup whole grain brown rice flour
2 TBS cornstarch
2 TBS nutritional yeast
3 TBS olive oil
1 TBS umeboshi plum vinegar

PREHEAT OVEN TO 375°F.

1. Mix ingredients together in a bowl by hand.

2. Roll out mixture to ¼" inch thickness on an oiled baking sheet or Silpat. With a plastic knife (to avoid damaging the Silpat), cut into squares. Dock crackers either by poking holes with a fork or by rolling with a docking tool.

3. Bake 12-15 minutes, until browned. Use care not to over-bake. Cool on baking surface until crisp.

Nutritional Information Per Serving
Servings 24 ✳ Calories 48 ✳ Fat 3g ✳ Protein 1g ✳
Carbohydrates 4g ✳ Cholesterol 0mg ✳
Sodium 109mg ✳ Fiber 0g

SESAME STICKS

Sesame seeds are full of calcium and protein. These crunchy snacks can be eaten as is, added to granola or put on top of salad instead of croutons. Press them through a cake decorator for professional looking sticks. These are fast to make and very tasty.

Ingredients

⅓ cup raw sesame seeds

1 tsp. salt

¼ cup raw sesame tahini

½ cup hot water

½ cup whole grain sorghum flour

¼ cup whole grain brown rice flour

¼ cup cornstarch

PREHEAT OVEN TO 375°F.

1. Toast sesame seeds in a dry frying pan on top of the stove on high heat. (You may want to cover the pan with a spatter screen, as the seeds pop when they toast.) Keep them moving while toasting. Toasting takes a few minutes.

2. In a food processor, combine the other ingredients and process until incorporated, scraping down the sides occasionally until dough forms a ball. Pulse in sesame seeds.

3. Place dough in a pastry bag with no tip, or in a plastic bag with the corner cut out. Mixture will be thick. Press out "sticks" about 2" long and ½" thick on a Silpat. Bake 22-25 minutes, until browned. Cool on Silpat or baking sheet. Store in an air-tight container.

Nutritional Information Per Serving

Servings 24 ✳ Calories 50 ✳ Fat 2g ✳ Protein 1g ✳
Carbohydrates 6g ✳ Cholesterol 0mg ✳
Sodium 79mg ✳ Fiber 1g

PRETZELS

Thin, salty pretzels — fun to make and even more fun to eat. Pipe these on a Silpat in any shape you'd like, or make traditional sticks.

Yeast Mixture
¼ cup water
½ tsp. yeast

Wet Ingredients
¼ cup plus 1 TBS water
1 tsp. Just Whites® or soy protein isolate powder
1 TBS sunflower oil
¼ tsp. rice vinegar
⅛ tsp. guar gum

Dry Ingredients
2 TBS sorghum flour
2 TBS tapioca flour
1 TBS potato flour
¼ cup arrowroot, cornstarch
 or potato starch
1½ tsp. organic cane sugar
⅛ tsp. xanthan gum
¼ tsp. salt

Kosher salt for decorating

PREHEAT OVEN TO 425°F.

1. In a measuring cup, heat water to 105° and then add yeast. Let it sit until foamy. Mix the other wet ingredients in a mixing bowl for 2 minutes on high speed until emulsified.

2. In a separate mixing bowl, whisk dry ingredients until incorporated. Add dry ingredients and yeast mixture to the bowl and mix 2 minutes on high speed.

3. Place dough in a pastry bag with a #230 tip, and pipe sticks 2" long on a Silpat or an oiled cookie sheet. Sprinkle with kosher salt. Cover with plastic wrap and let sticks rise in a warm place for 30-45 minutes. Bake for 15-20 minutes until golden brown.

Note: If you do not have a pastry bag, simply place the batter in a plastic bag and cut off a corner.

Nutritional Information Per Serving
Servings 32 ✳ Calories 43 ✳ Fat 1g ✳ Protein 0g ✳
Carbohydrates 8g ✳ Cholesterol 0mg ✳
Sodium 51mg ✳ Fiber 0g

CHERRY CHEWS

How about a perfect nutritious food, great for snacks or the lunchbox, easy to prepare, and keeps several months in the refrigerator or indefinitely in the freezer! Impossible? Not at all! These delicious, portable "chews" are made by dehydration — a food-preserving technique perfected by our ancestors - and today easily replicated with the oven. This recipe uses cherries, but you could use any fruit.

Ingredients

1 lb. bag frozen, dark, sweet, pitted cherries (thawed)

3 TBS agave nectar

1 tsp. cinnamon

PREHEAT OVEN TO 135°F.

1. Combine ingredients in a food processor and process to the consistency of applesauce. Strain mixture to remove excess liquid.

2. Use a Silpat or cut parchment paper to fit a baking sheet. Oil paper with walnut or sunflower oil and spread cherry mixture ¼" thick on paper-lined pan. Place in a 135° oven. If your oven's lowest temperature is 170°, set it to 170° and prop the door open 2".

3. Bake/dehydrate 6-8 hours. Chews are ready when the surface is dry and smooth. Use a plastic scraper to pry the chews from the cooking surface. While warm, imprint your favorite shapes with a cookie cutter and cut out with scissors. Or cut in strips for roll-ups.

Note: If you have a food dehydrator, chews can be made by placing the mixture on the smooth tray of a food dehydrator set at 135°.

Nutritional Information Per Serving
Servings 24 ✳ Calories 25 ✳ Fat 0g ✳ Protein 0g ✳
Carbohydrates 6g ✳ Cholesterol 0mg ✳
Sodium 0mg ✳ Fiber 0g

UME PLUM CASHEWS

It is simply amazing how good (and addicting) these are! The tangy, salty ume plum vinegar makes these nuts irresistible. And, a recipe couldn't get much easier than this one!

Ingredients

1 cup raw whole cashews
1 TBS ume plum vinegar

PREHEAT OVEN TO 350°F.

1. Place cashews in a glass pie pan and bake in the oven for 4 minutes. Stir and bake 4 more minutes.

2. Sprinkle ume plum vinegar on the nuts and stir until they are coated. Place in the oven for 1-2 minutes until the vinegar is evaporated.

3. Let cool and serve.

Nutritional Information Per Serving
Servings 8 ✳ Calories 167 ✳ Fat 14g ✳ Protein 5g ✳
Carbohydrates 8g ✳ Cholesterol 0mg ✳
Sodium 270mg ✳ Fiber 1g

SNACKING CEREAL WITH TOASTED ALMONDS

I love to snack, and cereal-based snacks take all of the guilt out of snacking. This low-fat, salty recipe reminds me of New Year's Eve celebrations of yesteryear when my mother made huge batches of a higher-calorie version of this recipe.

Ingredients

8 cups cereal (Health Valley Corn and Rice Crunch-Em's)

1 cup raw almonds

½ tsp. garlic salt
½ tsp. celery salt
½ tsp. garlic powder
½ tsp. onion powder

1 TBS GF Worcestershire sauce

Spray on olive oil

PREHEAT OVEN TO 250°F.

1. Combine spices in a large plastic bag.

2. Place cereal and almonds on a baking sheet and spray with spray-on oil. Transfer cereal and nuts to the plastic bag with the seasonings. Mix until coated.

3. Place the cereal and almonds back on the baking sheet and sprinkle on Worcestershire sauce (to taste). Bake 45 minutes, stirring every 15 minutes. Cool and enjoy!

Nutritional Information Per Serving
Servings 8 ✳ Calories 205 ✳ Fat 9g ✳ Protein 6g ✳ Carbohydrates 30g ✳ Cholesterol 0mg ✳ Sodium 410mg ✳ Fiber 4g

CAJUN CORN

Cajun seasoning can be purchased at most grocery stores. Check the ingredients to be sure it is gluten-free. This spice combination adds a tantalizing taste to the puffed corn and makes a healthy snack you can eat with reckless abandon. These are best right out of the oven, and are so quick to make, you'll make them often!

Ingredients

4 cups puffed corn cereal
1 TBS GF Cajun seasoning
Spray-on olive oil

PREHEAT OVEN TO 300°F.

Spread cereal on a cookie sheet. Generously spray with oil. Sprinkle Cajun seasoning to coat corn. Bake 10 minutes.

Nutritional Information Per Serving
Servings 4 ✳ Calories 50 ✳ Fat 0g ✳ Protein 1g ✳
Carbohydrates 14g ✳ Cholesterol 0mg ✳
Sodium 54mg ✳ Fiber 1g

TAMARI ALMONDS

This is a quick and nutritious treat to make when you need a salty snack fast. I like to make these to munch on during the 'big game'.

Ingredients

1 cup raw almonds
1 TBS wheat-free tamari

PREHEAT OVEN TO 350°F.

1. Place almonds in a glass pie pan and bake for 8 minutes.

2. Sprinkle tamari on the nuts and stir until they are coated. Place in the oven for 1 more minute until the tamari is evaporated.

3. Let cool and serve.

Nutritional Information Per Serving
Servings 8 ✳ Calories 105 ✳ Fat 9g ✳ Protein 4g ✳
Carbohydrates 4g ✳ Cholesterol 0mg ✳
Sodium 2mg ✳ Fiber 2g

ALTERNATIVE COOK, LLC™

BAKED RICE TORTILLA CHIPS

A low calorie, quick, tasty chip to serve with your favorite salsas. Seriously, I could live on these. They hit the spot every time.

Ingredients

1 cup brown rice flour
½ cup sorghum flour
½ cup tapioca flour
1 tsp. baking powder
2 tsp. xanthan gum
1 tsp. salt
1 cup warm water
3 TBS sunflower or olive oil

Garlic salt to taste

PREHEAT OVEN TO 350°F.

1. Whisk the flours, baking powder, salt and xanthan gum together. Separately mix water and oil together, then add to the flour mixture. Mix with hands or a pastry whisk until incorporated.

2. Oil hands and form dough into 8 "golf balls." Place plastic wrap over the bottom of a tortilla press and put a ball of dough on the plastic wrap. Place another piece of plastic wrap on top of the dough, close the press and slowly press down until the ball is flattened. (Or, roll the dough out on waxed paper with an oiled rolling pin.)

3. Heat an oiled cast iron pan or griddle and place the tortilla on it. Press it with a spatula while it is cooking. When browned, turn and cook the other side.

4. Cut tortillas into triangles and place on an oiled baking sheet. Spray with spray olive oil. Sprinkle with garlic salt. Bake 8 minutes or until golden brown.

Nutritional Information Per Serving
Servings 8 ✳ Calories 182 ✳ Fat 6g ✳ Protein 2g ✳
Carbohydrates 30g ✳ Cholesterol 0mg ✳
Sodium 331mg ✳ Fiber 1g

Breakfast Treats

People living a GFCF lifestyle often remark that breakfast is their biggest hurdle. Yes, there are lots of packaged cereals available in the natural food store, and combined with rice, nut or seed milk, make a great breakfast. But sometimes you want something different or special — like a breakfast treat! The recipes that follow will make you love breakfast again. Bake in batches and freeze in individual-serving freezer bags. Just take out of the freezer the night before and wake up to a breakfast you can dream about all night!

UPSIDE-DOWN COFFEE CAKE WITH WHIPPED TOPPING

UPSIDE-DOWN COFFE CAKE

Rich with pecans and a luscious whipped topping, this cake is a perfect partner for a steaming cup of freshly brewed rich coffee. It's always a welcomed addition to brunch or to serve for a very special holiday breakfast.

Dry ingredients

¾ cup whole grain sorghum flour

¾ cup whole grain brown rice flour

¼ cup plus 2 TBS cornstarch or tapioca flour

3 TBS arrowroot

¾ cup Sucanat® or brown sugar

1½ tsp. baking soda

¾ tsp. baking powder

⅜ tsp. salt

⅜ tsp. xanthan gum

Wet ingredients

3 egg whites

¼ cup plus 2 TBS sunflower oil or butter substitute

1 cup plus 3 TBS sparkling water

1½ tsp. vanilla

¾ tsp. rice vinegar

Crumble

3 TBS sunflower oil

½ cup Sucanat®

¾ cup chopped pecans

Tiny pinch of salt

PREHEAT OVEN TO 350°F.

1. Whisk dry ingredients together.

2. In a separate bowl, using hand mixer, beat wet ingredients for 1 minute. Add dry ingredients to wet ingredients and beat until incorporated.

3. In a separate bowl, mix the crumble.

4. Distribute crumble on the bottom of an oiled 8 x 8" (or smaller) baking pan. Pour batter on top. Bake 35-45 minutes, covering with parchment after 20 minutes to prevent over-browning. Remove from oven and cool. Run a knife around the edges, place a serving plate on top of the baking pan and flip cake on to the serving plate. Serve with **Whipped Topping** (Page 179).

Nutritional Information Per Serving
Servings 12 ✳ Calories 392 ✳ Fat 20g ✳
Protein 3g ✳ Carbohydrates 51g ✳ Cholesterol 0mg ✳
Sodium 358mg ✳ Fiber 2g

WHIPPED TOPPING

A very simple, tantalizing soy-free whipped topping to use on the Coffee Cake and a host of other things!

Ingredients
¼ cup butter substitute
⅓ cup confectioner's sugar
1 tsp. vanilla

1. Place ingredients in a blender, and process until incorporated.

2. Store extra topping up to seven days in an air-tight container in the refrigerator.

Nutritional Information Per Serving
Servings 8 ✳ Calories 70 ✳ Fat 6g ✳ Protein 0g ✳
Carbohydrates 5g ✳ Cholesterol 0mg ✳
Sodium 67mg ✳ Fiber 0g

GLAZED APPLE STICKY BUNS

There's nothing like the aroma of sticky buns baking in the oven! Family and friends will gather in the kitchen in eager anticipation when you bake a batch of these sweet, yummy breakfast treats.

Ingredients

1 recipe **Cinnamon Raisin Bread** batter (Page 142)

Sticky Bun Filling

2 apples, cored, peeled and grated

1 tsp. cinnamon

½ cup rice syrup

1 cup chopped pecans

3 TBS chopped candied ginger

¼ tsp. freshly grated nutmeg

Glaze

1 cup powdered sugar

1-2 TBS water

PREHEAT OVEN TO 400°F (When ready to bake.)

1. Turn oven on to 350° for 10 minutes, then turn it off.

2. Make **Cinnamon Raisin Bread** and turn dough onto an oiled work surface. Oil hands and a rolling pin and roll or pat dough into a rectangle approximately 9" wide by 12" long.

3. Combine Sticky Bun Filling ingredients in a bowl. Spread dough with filling. Roll up dough (like a jelly roll) and slice into 2" thick slices. Place slices side by side in an oiled 8 x 8" pan or nestle slices into the cups of an oiled muffin pan and place in the warmed oven with door closed.

4. Let rise until doubled in size. Remove from oven and preheat oven to 400°F.

5. Place buns back into oven and bake approximately 18-20 minutes, covering with parchment after 10 minutes to prevent over-browning. Combine glaze ingredients, adding more water if necessary (1 tsp. at a time) until "pour-able" consistency is achieved. Glaze while buns are warm.

Nutritional Information Per Serving

Servings 12 ✳ Calories 398 ✳ Fat 11g ✳ Protein 4g ✳ Carbohydrates 64g ✳ Cholesterol 0mg ✳ Sodium 182mg ✳ Fiber 3g

CHOCOLATE CHIP SCONES

These breakfast goodies have a wonderful, not-so-sweet taste and a wholesome, dry texture. If you don't like your scones with chocolate chips, substitute an equal amount of dried berries, raisins or chopped dried fruit(s).

Dry Ingredients

½ cup whole grain sorghum flour

½ cup Expandex™, cornstarch, tapioca flour or arrowroot

½ cup whole grain brown rice flour

1 tsp. xanthan gum

½ tsp. salt

⅓ cup organic cane sugar

½ cup GFCF chocolate chips

Wet Ingredients

¼ cup water

1 tsp. baking powder

½ tsp. baking soda

½ cup butter substitute

PREHEAT OVEN TO 375°F.

1. Sift the dry ingredients together in a bowl.

2. In a separate bowl, mix wet ingredients. Add wet to the dry ingredients. Using a pastry whisk, mix until small pea-sized morsels form. (This is a rather dry, crumbly dough.)

3. Turn mixture out on a Silpat or waxed paper. Oil hands with walnut or sunflower oil and pat out dough into a circle about 1" thick. Cut into triangles. Keep hands and knife oiled as you work with the dough.

4. Place scones on a Silpat or baking sheet and bake 20-25 minutes. Remove from oven and let cool on baking surface.

Nutritional Information Per Serving

Servings 12 ✳ Calories 215 ✳ Fat 12g ✳
Protein 1g ✳ Carbohydrates 26g ✳ Cholesterol 0mg ✳
Sodium 174mg ✳ Fiber 1g

"CHEESE" PUFFS

These light puffs make a great breakfast or can be used as a side for a soup or salad.
They resemble mini-popovers.

Dry Ingredients

½ cup white rice flour

½ cup potato starch

2 TBS organic cane sugar

¾ tsp. baking powder

½ tsp. salt

¼ tsp. xanthan gum

⅓ cup Spectrum, "Margarine" (Page 212) or dairy-free butter substitute

Wet Ingredients

2 egg whites

½ cup rice, nut or seed milk

½ cup non-dairy "cheddar cheese", grated, packed to measure

PREHEAT OVEN TO 400°F.

1. Place dry ingredients in a bowl and mix until incorporated.

2. In a separate bowl, mix egg whites and milk until frothy. Add dry ingredients to wet ingredients and mix with a mixer until completely incorporated.

3. Oil a mini-muffin pan and place batter in each cup.

4. Bake 20 minutes at 400°, turn the oven down to 350° and cover with parchment paper. Bake 10-15 more minutes. Cool before serving.

Nutritional Information Per Serving
Servings 24 ✳ Calories 62 ✳ Fat 3g ✳ Protein 2g ✳
Carbohydrates 2g ✳ Cholesterol 0mg ✳
Sodium 110mg ✳ Fiber 0g

ALTERNATIVE COOK, LLC™

POPOVERS

The best popovers are served right out of the oven, split in half and spread with a good butter substitute or your favorite jam. They are crusty on the outside and light and airy on the inside. Yum! It is worth the investment to purchase a non-stick popover pan. And, please refrain from opening the oven door to peek at them until just before the baking time is up — otherwise they don't puff up as high.

Cream
2 TBS raw finely chopped cashews
 Or raw hemp seeds
1 cup water

Wet Ingredients
8 egg whites
2 TBS sunflower oil
2 TBS butter substitute

Dry Ingredients
½ cup whole grain sorghum flour
¼ cup sweet rice flour
¼ cup cornstarch
½ tsp. salt

PREHEAT OVEN TO 450°F.

1. Add cashews or hemp seeds and water to a blender. Process until smooth. Pour into a mixing bowl and add wet ingredients. Whisk until incorporated.

2. In a separate bowl, whisk dry ingredients together. Add to wet ingredients and whisk until fully incorporated.

3. Oil a non-stick popover pan. Divide batter evenly into the pan.

4. Position baking rack one level below center. Put popovers in the oven and bake 20 minutes. Keep the oven door closed and turn oven down to 350° and bake 20-25 additional minutes. Cover with parchment paper and bake 25-35 minutes longer. Remove from oven and serve immediately. (These are very hot, handle carefully!)

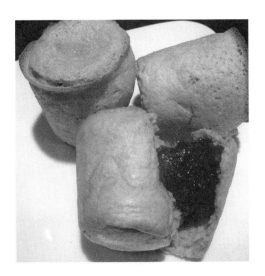

Nutritional Information Per Serving
Servings 12 ✳ Calories 106 ✳ Fat 6g ✳ Protein 3g ✳
Carbohydrates 11g ✳ Cholesterol 0mg ✳
Sodium 149mg ✳ Fiber 0g

GRANOLA

Homemade granola is ever so easy to make and gives you an opportunity to combine ingredients that work best for you and your family's dietary needs. Plus, it's so much cheaper and healthier! Be creative and have some fun! Try making granola with a variety of different dried fruits, seeds and nuts or with just a few. It lasts weeks when stored in an air-tight container and is so versatile as a topping for baked apples or your favorite fruit crisp.

Dry Ingredients
3 cups gluten-free oats (or buckwheat, quinoa or rice flakes)
½ cup raw slivered almonds
½ cup raw walnuts
½ cup raw sunflower seeds
¼ cup Sucanat®

Wet Ingredients
2 TBS sunflower oil
¼ cup GF rice syrup
1 tsp. cinnamon
¼ tsp. salt
1 tsp. vanilla

PREHEAT OVEN TO 250°F.

1. Mix dry ingredients in a bowl. In a saucepan combine first four wet ingredients. Bring to a boil and remove from heat; stir in the vanilla. Pour on top of the dry ingredients and stir until combined.

2. Spread granola out on a baking pan and bake 50 minutes, using a pancake turner to scrape up from pan and mix every 10 minutes to brown evenly. Cool and store in an air-tight container.

Nutritional Information Per Serving
Servings 18 ✳ Calories 140 ✳ Fat 8g ✳ Protein 5g ✳
Carbohydrates 13g ✳ Cholesterol 0mg ✳
Sodium 28mg ✳ Fiber 2g

ENGLISH MUFFINS

English Muffins are just delightful to eat for breakfast. These can be baked in an 11.5 oz. coffee can or in a stainless steel cylinder (available at cooking stores). Slice and toast, and spread with your favorite preserves. These make Sunday morning breakfast special.

Wet Ingredients
½ cup warm rice, nut or seed milk
¼ cup + 2 TBS warm water
1 TBS yeast
¼ cup sunflower oil
3 egg whites

Dry Ingredients
¾ cup whole grain sorghum flour
½ cup whole grain brown rice flour
½ cup potato starch
¾ tsp. xanthan gum
2 TBS organic cane sugar
1 tsp. salt

Cornmeal

PREHEAT OVEN TO 375°F (After bread rises.)

1. Prepare metal coffee can or stainless steel cylinder by oiling it and dusting it with cornmeal. Set aside.

2. Heat rice, nut or seed milk and water to 105°-110°F. Add yeast. Set aside until foamy.

3. Whisk dry ingredients together in a bowl. Separately, in a blender, process egg whites until foamy. With blender running, add oil in a slow steady stream until mixture thickens. Stir in yeast mixture. Add wet ingredients to dry ingredients and mix with mixer until smooth.

4. Place batter in cooking cylinder. Cover with plastic wrap so it is airtight. Move container to a warm place until mixture doubles in size.

5. Transfer container to oven and bake 40 minutes, covering with parchment after 20 minutes to prevent over-browning. (Do not under-bake.) Let cool and store in baking container with plastic wrap on top. Run knife around edges to remove. Slice and toast before serving.

Nutritional Information Per Serving
Servings 8 ✳ Calories 215 ✳ Fat 8g ✳ Protein 4g ✳
Carbohydrates 33g ✳ Cholesterol 0mg ✳
Sodium 296mg ✳ Fiber 2g

BOUNTIFUL BREAKFAST BITES

This combination of fruits, seeds and orange is simply wonderful. These not-so-sweet breakfast treats are packed with flavor and nutritious ingredients to start your day off right.

Flax Mix
1 tsp. flax seed
1½ TBS water

Wet Ingredients
¼ cup walnut or sunflower oil
1 tsp. vanilla
1 cup raisins
½ cup chopped Medjool dates
¼ cup chopped dried apples
2 TBS ground flax seeds
2 TBS toasted sesame seeds
1 TBS orange zest or 2 tsp. dried orange peel
½ cup sparkling water

Dry Ingredients
1 cup whole grain sorghum flour
¼ cup whole grain brown rice flour
¼ cup arrowroot
¼ cup almond meal
1½ tsp. baking powder
⅛ tsp. salt
½ cup date sugar

PREHEAT OVEN TO 350°F.

1. In a blender, combine flax seed and water. Process until smooth.

2. Whisk wet ingredients together in a bowl, then stir in Flax Mix.

3. In a separate bowl whisk dry ingredients together. Add to wet ingredients and stir until mixed.

4. Place paper muffin cups into a muffin pan and pour in batter – filling to the top of the muffin cups. Bake 27-29 minutes. Makes 8 muffins.

Nutritional Information Per Serving
Servings 8 ✳ Calories 338 ✳ Fat 11g ✳ Protein 6g ✳ Carbohydrates 60g ✳ Cholesterol 0mg ✳ Sodium 132mg ✳ Fiber 5g

BERRY GOOD CEREAL

Kids and grown-ups alike love cereal for breakfast. It's a staple item in our house, so I usually make a big batch of this and divide it into individual serving-size plastic bags for a quick "to go" breakfast.

Dry Ingredients

2 cups each:

  Health Valley Corn and Health Valley Rice Crunch-Em's

  Unsweetened Rice Puffs

  GF Millet Puffs

Wet Ingredients

2 TBS sunflower oil

¼ cup rice syrup

1 tsp. cinnamon

¼ tsp. freshly ground nutmeg

¼ tsp. salt

1 tsp. vanilla

1 cup freeze-dried fruit medley (such as Just Fruit Munchies®)

1 cup toasted, slivered almonds

PREHEAT OVEN TO 250°F.

1. In a saucepan, combine oil, rice syrup, cinnamon, nutmeg and salt. Bring to a boil and remove from heat; add vanilla. Stir in cereal and mix until combined.

2. Spread on an oiled baking pan and bake 30 minutes, stirring every 10 minutes to brown evenly.

3. After baked and cooled, add dried fruit medley and slivered almonds. Store in plastic bags or an airtight container.

Nutritional Information Per Serving

Servings 12 ✳ Calories 173 ✳ Fat 9g ✳ Protein 3g ✳ Carbohydrates 23g ✳ Cholesterol 0mg ✳ Sodium 146mg ✳ Fiber 2g

BAKED APPLES

Make this wholesome treat in the fall when apples are fresh-picked and abundant. Then make it again in the winter, and the spring, and the summer…well, you get the picture. For an extra-special treat, caramelize some sugar in a frying pan and drizzle over the apples.

Ingredients

4 apples, washed and cored, but not peeled

1 TBS walnut oil

2 tsp. cinnamon

1 cup almond meal

2 TBS organic cane sugar

Tiny pinch of salt

PREHEAT OVEN TO 400°F.

1. Place apples in a baking dish. Mix ingredients together and press into the core-hole of the apple.

2. Bake 45-50 minutes or until apples are soft. Serve warm or at room temperature.

Nutritional Information Per Serving
Servings 4 ✳ Calories 276 ✳ Fat 10g ✳ Protein 14g ✳ Carbohydrates 37g ✳ Cholesterol 0mg ✳ Sodium 2mg ✳ Fiber 4g

ALTERNATIVE COOK, LLC™

RICE PUDDING

What could be more comforting on a cold winter morning? This keeps well, so you can make it on Sunday and reheat it in individual servings every morning for a quick breakfast.

Ingredients

8 egg whites

2 cups vanilla rice milk

¼ cup raw tahini

4 cups leftover cooked rice (brown or white)

⅛ tsp. stevia OR ⅓ cup organic cane sugar

½ cup piñon nuts or sliced almonds

1 cup raisins

1 tsp. vanilla

¼ tsp. freshly ground nutmeg

1 tsp. cinnamon

PREHEAT OVEN TO 350°F.

1. Beat eggs until foamy. Add rice milk and tahini butter and beat until tahini butter is incorporated. Add other ingredients and mix until blended.

2. Place in oiled 8 x 8" baking pan. Bake 45-60 minutes. Serve warm or cooled.

Nutritional Information Per Serving
Servings 8 ✳ Calories 484 ✳ Fat 9g ✳ Protein 11g ✳
Carbohydrates 14g ✳ Cholesterol 0mg ✳ Sodium 89mg
✳ Fiber 3g

JELLY ROLL

A jelly roll is definitely worth the effort when you see the big eyes and hear the ooh's and aah's this breakfast elicits. Save this for a special occasion. This, the Chocolate Roll and the Flourless Chocolate Cake are the only recipes in the cookbook that call for egg yolks. A jelly roll is light, delicious and low-fat.

Wet Ingredients

4 eggs, separated

½ tsp. cream of tartar

¾ cup organic cane sugar or Florida Crystals®

2 tsp. vanilla

Dry Ingredients

¼ cup whole grain sorghum flour

¼ cup sweet rice flour

¼ cup cornstarch

1½ tsp. xanthan gum

1 tsp. baking powder

Tiny pinch of salt

½ cup raspberry or strawberry fruit spread

Confectioner's sugar for dusting

PREHEAT OVEN TO 400°F.

1. Prepare cookie sheet by lining with parchment, spraying with spray-on oil and lightly dusting with confectioner's sugar.

2. Separate egg whites and yolks. With the whisk attachment, beat the egg whites until foamy. Add cream of tartar and beat until stiff, gradually adding half of the sugar, one TBS at a time, and vanilla. Set aside.

3. In a separate bowl, whisk dry together ingredients.

4. Place egg yolks in a mixer with a paddle beater. Beat the yolks until thick and bright yellow, adding the remaining sugar. Fold yolk mixture into egg whites. Then fold in dry ingredients.

5. Spread about ¾" thick on prepared sheet. Bake 10-15 minutes until golden brown. Remove from oven and turn over on a new piece of parchment paper sprayed with oil and sprinkled with confectioner's sugar. Carefully remove baking parchment. Starting at shorter side, roll cake carefully. Let cool while rolled up.

6. Beat jelly in a bowl to spreading consistency. Carefully unroll cake and spread with jelly. Re-roll. Cover in plastic wrap and chill 2 hours. Slice and serve.

Nutritional Information Per Serving

Servings 10 ✳ Calories 166 ✳ Fat 2g ✳ Protein 3g ✳ Carbohydrates 35g ✳ Cholesterol 85mg ✳ Sodium 84mg ✳ Fiber 0g

FANTASTIC FRENCH TOAST

Homemade Cinnamon Bread is delicious made into French Toast, topped with pure, warmed maple syrup, dusted with confectioner's sugar and fresh berries on the side. You'll feel like you are being pampered at a resort hotel in your own home.

Ingredients

1 loaf of **Cinnamon Raisin Bread**
(Page 142)
6 egg whites
1 tsp. cinnamon
⅛ tsp. freshly ground nutmeg
⅓ cup rice, nut or seed milk

Pure maple syrup
Confectioner's sugar for dusting
Fresh berries

1. Slice **Cinnamon Raisin Bread** into 1" thick slices.

2. Whisk egg whites, cinnamon, nutmeg and milk in a bowl until egg whites are foamy.

3. Place one slice at a time in the egg mixture and saturate both sides. Place in a non-stick oiled skillet starting on high heat and turning down to medium. Flip to cook egg on both sides.

4. Place on plate and dust with confectioner's sugar. Decorate with fresh berries and serve with pure maple syrup.

Nutritional Information Per Serving
Servings 10 ✳ Calories 291 ✳ Fat 6g ✳ Protein 5g ✳
Carbohydrates 55g ✳ Cholesterol 0mg ✳
Sodium 278mg ✳ Fiber 2g

Tarts, Pies and Crisps

Pies bring back my favorite childhood memories of Sunday dinners. Our meal was served at 4 o'clock in the afternoon and it was usually topped off with pie worthy of a magazine cover.

Hazelnut Cream Pie with Chocolate Crust, 194

Berry Cream Tarts with Peach Glaze, 195

Apple Pie with Crumble Topping, 196

Peanut Butter Chocolate Pie (Vegan), 197

Orange Cream Pie with Chocolate Cookie Pie Crust (Vegan), 198

Mini Lemon Tarts, 200

Pumpkin Pudding Squares, 201

Cherry Crisp, 202

Apple Crisp, 203

"Ice Cream" Pie with Brownie Crust, 204

Banana Cream Pie with Meringue Icing, 206

Corn Flake Crust, 207

Vanilla Thins Pie Crust (Vegan), 208

Lemon "Zesties" Pie Crust (Vegan), 208

Perfect Pie Crust (Vegan), 209

HAZELNUT CREAM PIE WITH CHOCOLATE CRUST

If you haven't tried cream filling made from nuts yet, you are in for a treat! This wonderful pie is so good (and unique) you'll be proud to serve it. Nobody ever guesses the rich creamy filling is made with nuts!

Ingredients

½ cup raw cashews

½ cup hazelnuts

1½ cups water

2 tsp. vanilla

½ cup Frangelico Liquor

½ cup agave nectar

1 TBS kudzu

Tiny pinch of salt

2 tsp. agar powder

1 recipe **Chocolate Cookie Pie Crust** (Page 198)

Chocolate Bar (for shavings for top of pie)

1. Toast hazelnuts in oven for 8 minutes at 350°F.

2. Place hazelnuts and all other ingredients into a blender and process until smooth.

3. Strain mixture into a pot and bring to a boil whisking constantly. Turn heat down and whisk until mixture forms tracks or when it thickly coats the back of a spoon.

4. Pour into a **Chocolate Cookie Pie Crust.**

5. With a vegetable peeler, generously shave chocolate shavings on top of the pie. (Recommend: 70% Cocoa Scharffen Berger Chocolate Bar). Chill 3 hours before serving.

Nutritional Information Per Serving
Servings 8 ✳ Calories 417 ✳ Fat 26g ✳ Protein 5g ✳ Carbohydrates 46g ✳ Cholesterol 0mg ✳ Sodium 241mg ✳ Fiber 2g

BERRY CREAM TARTS WITH PEACH GLAZE

BERRY CREAM TARTS

Ingredients

1 recipe **Lemon "Zesties" Pie Crust** (Page 208)

Cashew Cream

1 cup raw cashews

1 cup water

½ cup Sucanat®

2 tsp. vanilla

⅛ tsp. ume plum vinegar

2 cups fresh blueberries, raspberries, strawberries

1. Make the **Lemon Zesties Pie Crust** and press into individual tart pans. Bake 15 minutes at 350°F to "set." Cool.

2. Place Cashew Cream ingredients in a blender and process until smooth. Taste and adjust for sweetness. Strain mixture into a pot and bring to a boil over high heat whisking constantly. Turn heat down and whisk until mixture forms tracks or when it thickly coats the back of a spoon.

3. Place cream filling in pre-baked crusts. Top with fresh berries. Glaze with Peach Glaze. Chill 2-3 hours and remove from tart pans before serving.

Nutritional Information Per Serving
Servings 8 ✳ Calories 464 ✳ Fat 27g ✳ Protein 7g ✳ Carbohydrates 53g ✳ Cholesterol 0mg ✳ Sodium 141mg ✳ Fiber 3g

PEACH (OR APRICOT) GLAZE

Ingredients

½ cup 100% fruit sweetened peach (or apricot) fruit spread

2 TBS water

1. Thin fruit spread with water and brush (dab) on the top of fruit tarts, being careful not to displace the berries.

Nutritional Information Per Serving
Servings 8 ✳ Calories 48 . Fat 0g ✳ Protein 0g ✳ Carbohydrates 13g ✳ Cholesterol 0mg ✳ Sodium 8mg ✳ Fiber 0g

APPLE PIE WITH CRUMBLE TOPPING

APPLE PIE

Ingredients

5 apples, peeled, cored and sliced

6 oz. can apple juice concentrate

1 cup raisins (optional)

1 tsp. cinnamon

½ tsp. freshly grated nutmeg

4 TBS cornstarch

1 recipe **Perfect Pie Crust** (Page 209)

PREHEAT OVEN TO 350°F.

1. Place ingredients (except cornstarch) in a large pot. Cover and simmer on medium heat for about 15 minutes.

2. Remove ½ cup of the apple-liquid and place into a measuring cup. Stir the cornstarch into the apple-liquid until dissolved and then stir it back into the large pot. Stir until thickened.

3. Make **Perfect Pie Crust**. Roll it out and place in a 9.5" oiled glass pie pan. Place apple filling in the crust.

4. Top with Crumble Topping. Bake on a baking sheet for 1 hour, covering with parchment paper after 30 minutes to prevent over-browning.

Nutritional Information Per Serving
Servings 8 ✳ Calories 376 ✳ Fat 14g ✳ Protein 7g ✳ Carbohydrates 60g ✳ Cholesterol 0mg ✳ Sodium 142mg ✳ Fiber 4g

CRUMBLE TOPPING

Ingredients

⅔ cup whole grain sorghum flour

¼ cup sunflower oil

1 tsp. cinnamon

½ cup slivered almonds

½ cup almond meal

½ cup Sucanat®

½ tsp. salt

1. Mix ingredients together, and sprinkle on the top of the apple pie before baking.

Nutritional Information Per Serving
Servings 8 ✳ Calories 230 ✳ Fat 14g ✳ Protein 6g ✳ Carbohydrates 23g ✳ Cholesterol 0mg ✳ Sodium 139mg ✳ Fiber 1g

PEANUT BUTTER CHOCOLATE PIE (VEGAN)

There are not too many flavor combinations more coveted than peanut butter and chocolate, and this creamy, chilled pie is a hit with both kids and adults. The corn flake crust gives it added texture. If you're like me – a chocoholic - double the chocolate chips. Who doesn't deserve a little decadence once in a while!

Ingredients

1 recipe of **Cornflake Crust** (Page 207)

⅓ cup warm water
2½ tsp. agar powder
½ cup creamy peanut butter
1 cup rice, nut or seed milk
⅓ cup rice syrup
2 TBS organic cane sugar
2 tsp. vanilla
1 TBS kudzu
½ tsp. salt

½ cup semi-sweet GF chocolate chips (reserve some to decorate the top of the pie)

1. Place agar and water in a blender and process until incorporated. Add the remaining ingredients except chocolate chips and blend until smooth.

2. Place the mixture into a pot. Whisk over high heat until mixture forms tracks or when it thickly coats the back of a spoon.

3. Place chocolate chips in a food processor and process to a fine chop. (This makes an easy-to-cut smooth layer of chocolate on the bottom of the pie.)

4. Make **Corn Flake Crust** and press into a 9" pie pan. Pre-bake crust 10 minutes. Turn oven off and place the processed chocolate chips on the bottom of the crust. Place back in the oven for 5 minutes or until melted.

5. Remove crust from oven and spread chocolate into an even layer. Add peanut butter filling. Decorate the top with chocolate chips. Refrigerate at least 2 hours and serve.

Nutritional Information Per Serving
Servings 8 ✳ Calories 359 ✳ Fat 20g ✳
Protein 10g ✳ Carbohydrates 40g ✳ Cholesterol 0mg ✳
Sodium 369mg ✳ Fiber 3g

ORANGE CREAM PIE WITH CHOCOLATE COOKIE PIE CRUST (VEGAN)

ORANGE CREAM PIE

This sounds a little different, doesn't it? It is tantalizing and slightly decadent at the same time. And, the colors are lovely — the orange cream accented by the brownie crust and shaved chocolate on top. This is a pie to serve to special guests.

Ingredients

½ cup warm water

2 tsp. agar powder

1 cup raw cashews

1 cup orange juice

2 TBS orange zest

½ cup Grand Marnier

A few drops orange oil (depending on taste and oil pungency)

½ cup agave nectar

1 tsp. vanilla

1 TBS kudzu

Chocolate Bar (for shavings for top of pie)

1. Dissolve agar powder in warm water until melted.

2. In a blender, add all of the ingredients and process until smooth. This may take several minutes.

3. Strain the mixture into a pot. Heat over high heat and bring to a boil whisking constantly. Turn heat down and whisk until mixture forms tracks or when it thickly coats the back of a spoon.

4. Make **Chocolate Cookie Pie Crust** and press into a 9" pie pan. Add orange cream filling.

5. With a vegetable peeler, generously top pie with chocolate shavings (Recommend: 70% Cocoa Scharffen Berger Chocolate bar). Chill 3 hours before serving.

Nutritional Information Per Serving

Servings 8 ✳ Calories 516 ✳ Fat 28g ✳ Protein 7g ✳ Carbohydrates 58g ✳ Cholesterol 0mg ✳ Sodium 243mg ✳ Fiber 3g

CHOCOLATE COOKIE PIE CRUST (VEGAN)

This pie crust recipe is made from the Chocolate Cookie recipe in this cookbook. It is easy to make, and tastes incredible. This is a crust to remember for any no-bake "icebox" pie filling. It uses half the recipe, about 10 cookies. No math involved - the ingredients listed below will give you a half recipe.

Ingredients

¼ cup butter substitute

½ recipe **Chocolate Cookies** (half recipe measurements follow)

Chocolate Cookie (Half recipe)

Flax Mix
⅓ cup water
1 TBS flax seed

Wet Ingredients

¼ cup sunflower oil
3 TBS of the Flax Mix (above)
½ tsp. liquid lecithin
1 tsp. vanilla

Dry Ingredients

¼ cup plus 2 TBS whole grain sorghum flour
2 TBS gafava or soy flour
¼ cup plus 2 TBS tapioca flour
¼ cup cocoa powder
½ cup organic cane sugar or xylitol
¾ tsp. xanthan gum
½ tsp. baking soda
¼ tsp. salt
2 TBS water

1. Bake cookies according to directions on Page 112. Cool.

2. Break cookies into a food processor and add the butter substitute. Process until cookies are crumbled and ingredients are incorporated.

3. Press into a 9" or 9.5" pie pan. Add filling. Refrigerate.

Nutritional Information Per Serving
Servings 8 ✳ Calories 220 ✳ Fat 14g ✳ Protein 1g ✳
Carbohydrates 25g ✳ Cholesterol 0mg ✳
Sodium 214mg ✳ Fiber 1g

MINI LEMON TARTS

If I need to bring something to an event, and don't have a lot of time to bake, this is my trusty standby dessert. People love these and they are fast and easy to make. Crumble a Lemon Chiffon Cake, and freeze it. Whenever you need a fast dessert, just dip into the crumbs. One cake makes enough crumbs for about 60 mini crusts. This recipe makes 12 tarts.

Crust

1 cup **Lemon Chiffon Cake** crumbs (Page 42)

1 TBS butter substitute

Lemon Filling

¼ cup warm water

1 tsp. agar powder

½ cup raw cashews or hemp seeds

¼ cup water

½ cup lemon juice

½ tsp. lemon oil (or a few drops, depending on the taste and oil pungency)

½ cup organic cane sugar

1 tsp. vanilla

1½ tsp. kudzu

Fresh lemon zest (to decorate top)

1. Place crust ingredients in a bowl and mix. Line a mini-muffin pan with paper liners. Fill each muffin cup with **Lemon Chiffon Cake** crumbs and press down to form a crust on the bottom and sides.

2. To make the filling, place ingredients in a blender and process until smooth. This may take 3-4 minutes. Strain mixture into a pot. Whisk constantly over high heat until mixture forms tracks or when it thickly coats the back of a spoon.

3. Pour into mini-crusts. Garnish with a zest of lemon on top. Refrigerate 2-3 hours before serving.

Nutritional Information Per Serving
Servings 12 ✳ Calories 141 ✳ Fat 7g ✳ Protein 3g ✳ Carbohydrates 19g ✳ Cholesterol 0mg ✳ Sodium 51mg ✳ Fiber g

PUMPKIN PUDDING SQUARES

Pumpkin is delicious year 'round, not just at Thanksgiving. These creamy pudding squares, with their gingerbread base, are a spicy alternative to pumpkin pie.

Ingredients

½ batch **Gingerbread Muffins**, crumbled (Measurements for a half-recipe follow. See directions for baking on Page 127.)

Pumpkin Pudding

1 can pumpkin

1 TBS kudzu

1 tsp. agar

⅓ cup maple syrup

½ cup rice, nut or seed milk

¾ tsp. cinnamon

¾ tsp. ginger

¼ tsp. cloves

¾ tsp. nutmeg

Gingerbread Muffins (Half recipe)
Dry Ingredients

¼ cup + 2 TBS teff flour

¼ cup brown rice flour

¼ cup + 2 TBS sorghum flour

1 tsp. baking powder

¼ tsp. salt

1 TBS ground flax meal

Wet Ingredients

2 TBS molasses

¼ cup rice, nut or seed milk

¼ cup sparkling water

2 TBS sunflower oil

1 egg white

¼ cup Sucanat®

½ tsp. ginger

½ tsp. cinnamon

¼ tsp. apple cider vinegar

1. Place pudding ingredients in a blender and process until smooth. Transfer ingredients to a pot. Heat over high heat, whisking constantly until mixture boils. Lower heat and stir a few minutes until thickened.

2. Oil an 8 x 8" pan and press crumbled gingerbread on the bottom of the pan about ½" thick. Spread Pumpkin Pudding on top and refrigerate 4 hours. Serve with **Whipped Cream** (Page 89).

Nutritional Information Per Serving

Servings 20 ✳ Calories 79 ✳ Fat 2g ✳ Protein 1g ✳ Carbohydrates 14g ✳ Cholesterol 0mg ✳ Sodium 60mg ✳ Fiber 1g

CHERRY CRISP

Warm just-out-of-the-oven fruit crisps on a chilly winter day are soul-satisfying indeed. Top them with GFCF vanilla frozen "ice cream" for a special treat. Crisps can be made with any kind of flaked grain (rice, quinoa, millet, buckwheat or gluten-free oats), nuts, seeds and spice. Experiment with different fruits. Reconstituted dried fruits boiled in juice make a rich, sweet filling when fresh fruits are no longer in season.

Ingredients
½ cup apple juice concentrate
¼ cup kirsch or juice or water
1 tsp. cinnamon
½ tsp. freshly ground nutmeg
3 TBS cornstarch
2 cups frozen pitted Bing cherries
2¼ cups **Granola** (Page 184)

PREHEAT OVEN TO 350°F.

1. Mix apple juice concentrate, kirsch, cinnamon, nutmeg and cornstarch in a pot and whisk over high heat until thickened. Remove from heat and stir in cherries.

2. Pour fruit into an oiled 6 x 7" glass baking pan or six individual serving ramekins. Top with **Granola.**

3. Bake 20-25 minutes, until bubbly. Cool slightly and serve.

Nutritional Information Per Serving
Servings 6 ✳ Calories 192 ✳ Fat 8g ✳ Protein 3.5g ✳
Carbohydrates 37g ✳ Cholesterol 0mg ✳
Sodium 21mg ✳ Fiber 3g

APPLE CRISP

This crisp contains all the wonderful flavors of an oatmeal cookie. It is a rich and oh-so-satisfying topping for apples.

Apple Ingredients

6 peeled, cored and chopped apples

½ cup raisins

1 cup apple juice concentrate

1 tsp. cinnamon

¼ tsp. fresh ground nutmeg

¼ cup cornstarch

Crisp

¼ cup rice syrup

1 TBS walnut or sunflower oil

2 TBS water

¼ cup applesauce (no sugar added)

1½ tsp. egg substitute* plus 4 TBS water

½ cup date sugar

½ tsp. vanilla

¼ cup plus 2 TBS whole grain sorghum flour

¼ cup plus 2 TBS whole grain brown rice flour

¼ tsp. baking soda

¾ tsp. cinnamon

¼ tsp. salt

1½ cups flaked grain (rice, quinoa, buckwheat, millet, gluten-free oats)

¼ cup slivered almonds

PREHEAT OVEN TO 350°F.

1. Place first 5 Apple ingredients into a pot and simmer over low heat about 20 minutes, or until the apples are soft.

2. Remove ½ cup of liquid and mix with cornstarch until blended. Add cornstarch mixture back into pot and whisk until mixture thickens. Set aside.

3. Mix Crisp ingredients in a stand mixer. Place cooked apples in an 11½ x 8" oiled baking pan. Distribute Crisp topping over the apples. Bake 22-25 minutes. Cool slightly and serve.

Note: EnerG® Brand egg substitute works well in this recipe.

Nutritional Information Per Serving
Servings 12 ✳ Calories 254 ✳ Fat 5g ✳ Protein 5g ✳
Carbohydrates 51g ✳ Cholesterol 0mg ✳
Sodium 32mg ✳ Fiber 6g

"ICE CREAM" PIE
WITH BROWNIE PIE CRUST

"ICE CREAM" PIE

Sweet, creamy and totally sinful – "ice cream" laced with chopped chocolate covered almonds resting on a bed of brownies. This could become your favorite pie!

Ingredients

1½ pints (24 oz) non-dairy Vanilla "ice cream"*

½ cup dark chocolate covered almonds (reserve some for top of pie)

1 recipe **Brownie Pie Crust** (Page 205)

1. Place ice cream on a cutting board and chop into large pieces with a butcher knife. Add chopped almonds and chop almonds into "ice cream" to incorporate.

2. Place mixture in **Brownie Pie Crust** and sprinkle top with chocolate covered almonds. Place pie in freezer until 30 minutes before you are ready to serve. Let it defrost 30 minutes before cutting and serving.

*Recommend: Rice Dream® Vanilla

Nutritional Information Per Serving
Servings 8 ✳ Calories 420 ✳ Fat 26g ✳ Protein 5g ✳
Carbohydrates 47g ✳ Cholesterol 0mg ✳
Sodium 90mg ✳ Fiber 3

BROWNIE PIE CRUST

What could possibly be better than a crust made of brownies with added chocolate chips? This is one of the best complements to any no-bake pie filling you'll ever find.

Ingredients

One recipe **Mini Brownies** (Page 73), baked in an 8 x 8" pan for 25 minutes

½ cup mini chocolate chips, or shaved, semi-sweet chocolate bar

1. Crumble brownies in a bowl. (Note: if the tops and corners are too hard to crumble, remove from bowl to snack on.) Add mini chocolate chips or chocolate shavings.

2. Press into a 9" glass pie pan and fill with your favorite no-bake pie filling. Refrigerate and serve.

Nutritional Information Per Serving

Servings 8 ✳ Calories 240 ✳ Fat 15g ✳ Protein 3g ✳
Carbohydrates 27g ✳ Cholesterol 0mg ✳
Sodium 53mg ✳ Fiber 2g

BANANA CREAM PIE
WITH MERINGUE TOPPING

Sweet bananas in a rich, luscious cream filling, with a vanilla cookie crust, topped with thick foamy, perfectly-browned meringue. This pie presents an array of mouth-feel delectable to anyone's palate.

Ingredients

1 recipe **Vanilla Thins Pie Crust**
(Page 208)

Macadamia Nut Cream

1½ cups raw or dry roasted (unsalted) macadamia nuts

1½ cups water

½ cup organic cane sugar

¼ cup Sucanat®

2 tsp. vanilla

½ tsp. ume plum vinegar

1 tsp. agar powder

1 TBS kudzu

4-5 ripe bananas, sliced

Meringue Icing (Page 60)

1. Make the **Vanilla Thins Pie Crust** and press into a 9" or 9.5" glass pie pan. Bake 15 minutes at 350°F to "set." Cool.

2. Place Macadamia Nut Cream ingredients in a blender and process until smooth. Taste and adjust for sweetness. Strain mixture into a pot and bring to a boil over high heat whisking constantly. Turn heat down and whisk until mixture forms tracks or when it thickly coats the back of a spoon.

3. Remove from heat and add bananas. Pour into pie crust. Refrigerate 2 hours.

4. Pipe **Meringue Icing** on top and place under the broiler for 3-5 minutes until meringue is golden brown.

Nutritional Information Per Serving
Servings 12 ✳ Calories 387 ✳ Fat 21g ✳
Protein 6g ✳ Carbohydrates 50g ✳ Cholesterol 0mg ✳
Sodium 111mg ✳ Fiber 4g

ALTERNATIVE COOK, LLC™

CORN FLAKE CRUST

If you have a few good pie crusts in your repertoire, you'll be empowered to mix and match them into many different sweet and savory creations. Pre-bake this crust and fill with your favorite no-bake filling.

Dry Ingredients
1½ cups GF corn flakes
½ cup sorghum flour
1 TBS organic cane sugar

Wet Ingredients
½ cup smooth or crunchy peanut butter
½ tsp. salt
3 TBS water

PREHEAT OVEN TO 350°F.

1. Place cereal and flour in a food processor and process until cereal is coarsely ground. Add other ingredients and process until it starts to stick together.

2. Firmly press into an oiled 9.5" glass pie plate.

3. Bake 10-15 minutes. Fill with no-bake pie filling. Refrigerate and serve.

Nutritional Information Per Serving
Servings 8 ✳ Calories 157 ✳ Fat 9g ✳ Protein 5g ✳
Carbohydrates 17g ✳ Cholesterol 0mg ✳
Sodium 265mg ✳ Fiber 2g

VANILLA THINS PIE CRUST (VEGAN)

Ingredients
1 recipe **Vanilla Thins** (Page 108)

2 TBS sunflower oil or raw tahini butter
2 TBS organic cane sugar
¼ cup almond meal or ground hemp seed

1. Crumble cookies into a food processor. Add other ingredients and process until the mixture clumps.

2. Press into an oiled 9.5" pie pan or individual pie pans. Fill with any refrigerated filling.

> **Nutritional Information Per Serving**
> Servings 8 ✳ Calories 253 ✳ Fat 12g ✳ Protein 4g ✳ Carbohydrates 34g ✳ Cholesterol 0mg ✳ Sodium 135mg ✳ Fiber 1g

LEMON "ZESTIES" PIE CRUST (VEGAN)

The lemony tang of this pie crust pairs nicely with vanilla cream fillings and fruit.

Ingredients
1 recipe **Lemon "Zesties"** (Page 107)

¼ cup butter substitute
2 TBS organic cane sugar
½ tsp. dried lemon peel
¼ cup puffed grain cereal (rice or millet)

PREHEAT OVEN TO 350°F.

1. Place cereal into a food processor and process until powdered.

2. Crumble cookies and add them along with all other ingredients to the food processor.

3. Process until the mixture clumps.

4. Press into an oiled 9.5" pie pan, or into individual pie pans. Cover with parchment paper and bake 15-20 minutes. Let cool. Fill with any refrigerated filling.

> **Nutritional Information Per Serving**
> Servings 8 ✳ Calories 248 ✳ Fat 13g ✳ Protein 1g ✳ Carbohydrates 33g ✳ Cholesterol 0mg ✳ Sodium 100mg ✳ Fiber 1g

ALTERNATIVE COOK, LLC™

PERFECT PIE CRUST (VEGAN)

When my favorite options — a cake, cookie, brownie or cereal-based crust - isn't right for the recipe, this is an "everyday" pie crust recipe you can use universally. It works equally well with baked and no-bake fillings. The crust is a little bit salty, perfect for a savory filling and a wonderful compliment for a sweet pie filling.

Dry Ingredients

Single Crust	Double Crust
¼ cup	½ cup garbanzo bean flour
¼ cup	½ cup whole grain sorghum flour
¼ cup	½ cup tapioca flour or Expandex™
¼ cup	½ cup white rice flour
¼ tsp.	½ tsp. guar gum
¾ tsp.	1½ tsp. salt

Wet Ingredients

Single Crust	Double Crust
¼ cup	½ cup butter substitute
3 TBS	⅓ cup water

PREHEAT OVEN TO 350°F.

1. Place butter substitute and water in a food processor. Add the dry ingredients. Pulse until barely incorporated. (Do not over mix). If making a double crust, divide dough in half. Wrap rounds in plastic and refrigerate 1 hour.

2. For a single pie crust, roll out dough with an oiled rolling pin. Flip dough into an oiled 9" or 9.5" glass pie pan. Place parchment paper on top of the dough, and cover with pie weights or dry beans (to weight the crust down while baking).

3. Bake 20-25 minutes. Remove parchment and dry beans or pie crust weights.

4. If making a double-crusted pie, omit pre-baking. Roll out crusts and fill. Spray the top with spray oil and bake according to the directions for the pie.

Nutritional Information Per Serving
Servings 8 ✳ Calories 126 ✳ Fat 6g ✳ Protein 2g ✳
Carbohydrates 16g ✳ Cholesterol 0mg ✳
Sodium 68mg ✳ Fiber 0g

Elementary Essentials

Nuts, seeds, alternative milks, meals and margarine play an essential role in many of the recipes in this cookbook. Let's take a minute to learn the right technique to make them so they can contribute positively to the texture and flavors of the finished baked goods.

BLANCHED NUTS

Blanching nuts enables you to easily remove their skins. Blanching is not necessary, but is often done to yield a "lighter" cream or milk when used in a sauce. (Almonds are the most fun to blanch, because popping the skins off is just good clean fun!) Once blanched, you can let them dry and use them as is, or you can toast them.

Ingredients
Raw nuts

1. Place several inches of water in a pot and bring to a boil.

2. Add nuts and boil one minute.

3. Strain nuts and place on several layers of paper towels.

4. "Pop" off the skins.

5. Dry the nuts again on fresh paper towels.

TOASTED NUTS

Toasting nuts brings out a delicious flavor and adds crunch. The trick is to toast them "just enough" but not too much. They get crunchy as they cool.

Ingredients
Raw almonds, walnuts, cashews, pecans, hazelnuts or piñon (pine) nuts

PREHEAT OVEN TO 350°F.

1. Place nuts on a dry baking sheet or glass pie plate and place in the oven for 8 minutes (except hazelnuts which need to bake 12 minutes). Lighter nuts such as cashews and piñons need to be stirred halfway into the baking time.

2. Remove from oven, cool and use in the recipe.

TOASTED SEEDS

Toasting seeds is easy, and brings out phenomenal flavor and aroma. If I'm having company and I want my house to smell unusually delicious — (while some people heat olive oil with garlic or bake cookies) — I toast seeds.

Ingredients
Sesame seeds, pumpkin seeds, sunflower seeds or hemp seeds

1. Place seeds in a dry saucepan and place on the stove on high heat. Keep pan moving around until seeds are puffed and lightly browned. If toasting sesame seeds, cover the pan with a spatter screen used for frying to prevent seeds from popping out of the pan.

2. Cool and use in recipes.

"MARGARINE"

This recipe contains no hydrogenated oils and no tropical oils (palm fruit, palm kernel or coconut) as do many store-bought varieties of "dairy-free" margarine. The optional ingredients —GF butter flavor and food colorings — are purely for aesthetics. The butter flavor tends to bake out, and I prefer to use this margarine just in baking rather than as a table spread. Did you know that when margarine was first introduced it was white? Later, by popular demand, it was colored yellow to look more like butter.

Ingredients
⅓ cup plus 2 TBS water
½ tsp. xanthan gum
½ tsp. salt
⅓ cup sunflower or canola oil
¹⁄₁₆ tsp. citric acid

Optional
1 tsp. butter flavor
3 drops natural yellow food coloring
2 drops natural orange food coloring

1. Place ingredients into a food processor and process until smooth and creamy (about 1 minute). Store in refrigerator in an airtight container and use within seven days. Do not freeze.

2. This recipe yields about ⅔ cup "margarine" and can be substituted for oil in any of the baked recipes in this cookbook. If a recipe also calls for xanthan or guar gum, omit them from the recipe since gum is already present in the "margarine."

Note: If using a pre-packaged GF mix that contains xanthan or guar gum, using this "margarine" is not the best choice. The recipe will contain too much gum and the end product will be "rubbery." Use oil instead.

Nutritional Information Per Serving
Servings 18 ✳ Calories 36 ✳ Fat 4g ✳ Protein 0g ✳
Carbohydrates 0g ✳ Cholesterol 0mg ✳
Sodium 59mg ✳ Fiber 0g

NUT OR SEED MILK

Make this as a substitution for milk – I prefer using "whole" milk in baking.

One Cup "Skim" Milk
8 raw nuts or 4 tsp. seeds
1 cup water
1 tsp. maple syrup (optional, to taste)
Tiny pinch of salt (optional)

One Cup "Whole" Milk
16 raw nuts or 8 tsp. seeds
1 cup water
1 tsp. maple syrup (optional, to taste)
Tiny pinch of salt (optional)

1. Place ingredients in blender and blend 2-3 minutes until smooth. Strain. Makes 1 cup.

2. Store in refrigerator and use within 1-2 days.

Nutritional Information Per Serving
Skim
Servings 1 ✳ Calories 45 ✳ Fat 3g ✳ Protein 1g ✳
Carbohydrates 4g ✳ Cholesterol 0mg ✳
Sodium 8mg ✳ Fiber 1g
Whole
Servings 1 ✳ Calories 90 ✳ Fat 6g ✳ Protein 2g ✳
Carbohydrates 8g ✳ Cholesterol 0mg ✳
Sodium 16mg ✳ Fiber 1g

NUT OR SEED MEAL

Usually as little as ¼ cup is plenty to fortify a recipe with protein and fiber.

Ingredients
½ cup raw nuts or seeds

1. Place nuts or seeds in a coffee or spice grinder (dedicated to making nut/seed meal) or food processor and process into a fine meal.

2. Use immediately in the recipe. If you have leftovers, add to a smoothie, or store in an airtight container for up to one week.

Note: Making it right when you need it ensures freshness and saves a lot of money. Nuts and seeds can go rancid, so store them in the refrigerator or freezer and grind them when you need them. Use only raw nuts or seeds – not those with oil added, since processing turns them into nut/seed butter! If you use raw and accidentally add moisture (water) or oil, you'll also get butter. If this happens, add some salt and enjoy it on a cracker! If a recipe calls for ¼ cup nut or seed meal, start by grinding ½ cup whole nuts or seeds. This is a "rule of thumb" yet varies depending on the size of the nut.

ALTERNATIVE COOK, LLC™

HELP AND SUPPORT

The number of children and adults following a gluten-free and casein-free lifestyle grows daily. Some individuals live in metropolitan areas where GFCF foods and support services are plentiful, while others live in rural communities without even the most basic options available. Even the most determined person can run out of motivation from time to time, or need additional information/education on particular aspects of this lifestyle. The good news is that help and support is often no farther away than a telephone call or the click of your mouse. There's a whole community of individuals ready, willing and able to help.

The Alternative Cook's website: **www.alternativecook.com**

Here you'll find a wealth of information on cooking and baking GFCF, plus ways to connect with other individuals who live this lifestyle. At our website you can:

* Find recipes, tips and ideas when your own creativity is bottoming out.

* Sign up for our regular newsletter on cooking and baking GFCF.

* Join our online community and participate on Jean's blog and post your own question or comment.

* Find helpful sources for purchasing GFCF specialty items.

* Read articles and gain insight to the diet and lifestyle.

* Get help converting a favorite recipe.

* Learn about selling this cookbook or the DVDs as a fund-raiser for your organization.

Explore our full-length cooking DVDs and online video streams. The DVDs guide you, step-by-step, in making delicious foods gluten and casein free. Mexican, Italian, Kids' Meals and Chocolate are available. It's like having a GFCF cooking instructor in your very own home and you don't need a DVD player in the kitchen. DVDs come with a recipe booklet.

We'd love to hear from you about your GFCF baking experiences and using this cookbook. We all have our stories to share, the "I can't believe this is GFCF!" praise, and the "near misses" (or complete misses!) that make baking GFCF always a little bit of a walk on the wild side. You're never alone in this adventure – reach out and connect with us and "Remember, there is always an alternative."™

Many national and local organizations exist that support individuals through education and information on following a special diet. Some are general health organizations while others have a more specific focus, like Autism or Celiac Disease. Many have local chapters.

American Academy of Asthma and Immunology	www.aaaai.org
American Academy of Dermatology	www.aad.org
American Celiac Disease Alliance	www.americanceliac.org
American College of Allergy, Asthma and Immunology	www.acaai.org
American Diabetes Association	www.diabetes.org
American Dietetic Association	www.eatright.org
American Heart Association	www.americanheart.org
American Medical Association	www.ama-assn.org
Anaphylaxis Canada	www.anaphylaxis.org
Arthritis Foundation	www.arthritis.org
Ask a GFCF	www.askagfcf.com
Ask Alternative Cook	www.askaltcook.com
Asthma and Allergy Foundation of America	www.aafa.org
Attention Deficit Disorder Association	www.add.org
Autism Network for Dietary Intervention	www.autismndi.org
Autism Research Institute	www.autism.com
Autism Society of America	www.autism-society.org
Autism Speaks	www.autismspeaks.org
Celiac Disease Foundation	www.celiac.org
Celiac Sprue Assn, USA	www.csaceliacs.org
Celiac.com	www.celiackids.com
Crohn's and Colitis Foundation of America	www.ccfa.org
Feingold® Association of the United States	www.feingold.org
Food Allergy & Anaphylaxis Network	www.foodallergy.org
Food Allergy Initiative	www.foodallergyinitiative.org
Gluten Free / Dairy Free Diet	www.gfcf.diet.org
Gluten Intolerance Group® of North America	www.gluten.net
Great Gluten Escape Camp for Kids	www.dallasrock.org/gge.htm
International Foundation for Functional GI Disorders	www.iffgd.org
Jean Duane's GFCF Blog	www.askjeanduane.com
National Foundation for Celiac Awareness	www.celiacawareness.org
Nat'l Inst. of Diabetes, Digestive & Kidney Diseases	www.niddk.nih.gov
Skin Cancer Foundation	www.skincancer.org
Talk About Curing Autism (TACA)	www.talkaboutcuringautism.org
University of Chicago Celiac Disease Center	www.celiacdisease.net
University of Maryland Center for Celiac Research	www.celiaccenter.org

Index

ALTERNATIVE COOK, LLC™

INVITE JEAN DUANE TO
SPEAK AT YOUR NEXT EVENT!

Jean Duane, Alternative Cook is a frequent speaker at events around the country, and is available to speak at conferences, seminars, support groups, grocery stores – anyplace people interested in living a healthy, GFCF lifestyle congregate or gather together to learn.

Ms. Duane makes cooking with alternative foods fun, interesting and best of all… delicious! Attendees leave feeling excited about their new-found confidence and the new recipes, new ideas, and new techniques they can add to their repertoire. She provides valuable information on how to "think alternatively"' about cooking that doesn't end when the seminar does. Jean's blog allows attendees to stay connected and share their successes, innovations (and yes, mishaps!) with each other.

Jean's presentations combine her signature style of education, entertainment and empowerment in the kitchen that characterizes everything she does.

Visit **www.alternativecook.com** to contact Jean.